PETER BAKES

PETER SAWKINS

PETER BAKES

PETER SAWKINS

Photography by Susie Lowe

BLACK & WHITE PUBLISHING

First published 2021
by Black & White Publishing Ltd,
Nautical House, 104 Commercial Street, Edinburgh, EH6 6NF

1 3 5 7 9 10 8 6 4 2   21 22 23 24

ISBN: 978 1 78530 350 0

A CIP catalogue record for this book is available from the British Library.

Design by Richard Budd Design
Printed and bound by Bell & Bain Ltd., Glasgow

To my flatmates and family —
the people with whom I have loved
sharing all the excitement of these
baking adventures.

CONTENTS

1 – BASICS 13

2 – CAKES 57

3 – PASTRY 85

BEFORE THE RECIPES

ABOUT ME AND BAKING

I'm Peter. I'm a badminton-mad, accounting and finance student and an obsessive home baker. I have baked for as long as I can remember. It started in the kitchen with packet cupcake mixes, flapjacks and shortbread. Then, when I was 12, I got completely hooked on the third series of the *Great British Bake Off*. Our family had watched and enjoyed the previous two series, but this series sparked an intense fascination with the process of baking. I think this was largely driven by the enthusiasm of James Morton and John Whaite, two young men with an unapologetic passion for this hobby. These role models gave me the confidence to explore baking without worrying what anyone else would think (but, as an aside, people always support your baking hobby because they love to eat cake!). After this, I became a little obsessed! I watched and rewatched *Bake Off* episodes, the *Bake Off* masterclasses, *Great British Menu*, *Saturday Kitchen*, *Masterchef* and anything else foodie on TV and tried to replicate the techniques I saw. My baking book collection grew a little out of hand, and I would combine different recipes to test out as many new techniques as possible.

As I was having fun experimenting, failing frequently and improving a lot, I didn't realise I was, in a sense, training for the show that inspired me to love baking. I applied for *Bake Off* when I was 17, didn't get on, applied again when I was 19 and was accepted. Baking had had a significant impact on the previous eight years of my life, so the chance to take part in *Bake Off*, my original inspiration, was beyond exciting!

We shot the show in the middle of the first UK Covid-19 lockdown, so we lived and baked in this surreal, intense and lively 'Baking Bubble' for seven brilliant weeks. I had the most amazing time, met the most amazing people and, at the end, was fortunate enough to win.

Bake Off plays a huge part in this book. Without *Bake Off*, I would never have written it, and for that reason and so many more, I am incredibly grateful to have been given this opportunity.

After the show, I had many interviews with journalists asking what was 'next' for me and often that included the question of whether I would write a book. I'd always said I didn't think I'd be writing a book any time soon, but clearly that changed quickly when Ali from Black & White Publishing got in touch and we talked through how *Peter Bakes* might come about. The idea took root and, I must admit, rather soon it became an opportunity I couldn't turn down. Creating this book, alongside completing a tough year at university, has been challenging and busy but incredibly rewarding. My recipes mean a lot to me, so it is a complete joy to see them come to life on the page, along with Susie Lowe's incredible photography. The prospect of you reading my words and trying out my recipes here in this book is all at once stupendously exciting and incredibly nerve-racking!

A QUESTION OF AUTHORITY!

I have eaten, slept and breathed home baking for a significant proportion of my life and I have put a lot of time and energy into learning about and practising the subject. However, I am by no means a trained professional. In other words, I am not an authority. This made me quite concerned to be clear about how I have framed the writing of this book and to share that with you transparently. *Peter Bakes* is simply me sharing the style of baking that I have loved and practised throughout the past nine years. The techniques I share are the techniques I have learned and adapted from a wide range of TV shows and books and that I personally find success with in the kitchen. The recipes are ones that I get excited about writing, baking and eating. So, I'm not a baking authority, but I am an authority in the baking style of Peter Sawkins, and that is what I am excited to share with you here.

THE PURPOSE OF *PETER BAKES*

Cookery books serve many different purposes; these have influenced how I thought about putting this book together. Of course, I believe the recipes to be essential, and my wish is for you to discover many different recipes that capture your interest, inspire you to get busy in the kitchen and that you'll revisit time and time again. You'll see that I have included a Basics chapter, which I hope will provide you with some simple base recipes that you can use and build on to create bakes of your own. But I don't think recipe books should be entirely prescriptive, and so if you want to mix and match recipes or make your own changes, then absolutely go for it. Scribble in personal notes and reminders; I won't get mad at you for amending my recipes or for writing on the pages of this book!

It's a great joy and comfort of mine to sit down with a cookery book and flick through the pictures, read some excerpts and soak up a bit of inspiration for future bakes. I can easily get lost in the story and imagery of a beautiful cookbook. It can create a real sense of escapism, making for a very relaxing evening! And so, we try to create here something you can take pleasure from and connect with when on a short break from your day, whether through a quick skim or a longer read as you plan future bakes.

Food connects us with so many people, places and memories; recipes often hold great stories within. I love hearing about other people's connections with food, and I share here some stories of my own, where one exists. These wee stories make me smile and remind me how special the process of baking is. Recipe introductions might feature my personal connections with that particular bake, or they might include valuable technical points. So, even if you're not a fan of gushy stuff about my emotional relationship with sugary treats, you still might take a moment to read the odd intro so you can pick up some more practical hints and tips.

Along with being something enjoyable to look at, sit with and read, a cookbook needs to be used. I would find it incredibly flattering if your copy of *Peter Bakes* gradually got covered in flour and egg, was scribbled all over with pencil markings and had dog-eared, well-thumbed pages. I don't think you should be precious about a cookbook!

IS THIS BOOK GLUTEN-FREE?

My brother has had to live with a gluten-free diet for the past 13 years. This means, right from the moment I became a baking obsessive, I had to bake gluten-free to make sure the biggest eater in the family could help get rid of cake! It was essential to me that this book be accessible for gluten-free bakers. However, now I no longer live with my brother, most of my baking is not gluten-free, so I also wanted to represent that. The compromise is quite simple: all the recipes here are written as standard, but every single one has gluten-free amendments, so you can make identical bakes whether you are gluten-free or not. So, I don't call this a gluten-free book, but it can be if you want!

Gluten-free baking need not be complicated, scary or confusing. I don't create complicated flour blends, and the vast majority of ingredients are readily available in your standard supermarket, big or small. Techniques are largely unchanged, and all of your classic baking skills are directly transferable to gluten-free bakes. I'd love for my gluten-free friends to find these recipes exciting and to have the chance to maybe try out a new bake that you've rarely been able to enjoy before. And, likewise, I hope my non-gluten-free readers will find this book a valuable tool when the opportunity arises to bake for your gluten-free friends.

Thank you so much for picking up my book and giving my recipes a go. It is hugely meaningful to me. I hope you enjoy!

With big baking love,

Peter

NOTES ON EQUIPMENT, INGREDIENTS AND TECHNIQUES

EQUIPMENT

The following items of equipment are what I consider to be the most useful for baking and would make for a very well kitted-out kitchen ready to bake virtually anything.

- **Stand mixer** – This is an expensive piece of kit, but if you're a big fan of baking, it really is the best tool to take your creations to the next level.

- **Electric hand whisk** – Anything a stand mixer can do, an electric hand whisk can do too. It just requires a little more work from you, takes a bit longer and can be more fiddly as you are without free hands.

- **Flexible spatulas** – I rarely use wooden spoons. Instead I use flexible spatulas as these are terrific for folding ingredients gently, stirring and scraping out every last bit of batter from a bowl.

- **Palette knives** – I like having three sizes of palette knife; a small 10cm, a medium 15cm and a large 25cm. These are great for icing cakes, levelling off mousses or batters and for lifting and moving delicate cakes and pastries.

- **Measuring spoons** – A set of measuring spoons ranging from ¼ teaspoon to 1 tablespoon is vital.

- **Balloon whisks** – I like to use a sturdy metal balloon whisk for whipping cream and a silicone one to whisk crème pat while cooking in a non-stick pan.

- **Mixing bowls** – A selection of three sizes and different mixing bowl materials is useful. I like using metal, pyrex and earthenware. Metal is perfect for chocolate work; pyrex is ideal as something that can be put in the microwave, and earthenware is a terrific all-rounder.

- **Digital sugar thermometer** – These cost about £10 online and are valuable tools for Italian meringue, curds, custards, and more.

- **Piping bags** – Piping is a quick and clean way of distributing batters and decorating bakes. You can find biodegradable disposable piping bags online.

- **Cake tins** – The selection listed below will allow you to bake most recipes in this book:

    2 x 18cm deep cake tins
    2 x 20cm deep cake tins
    1 x 20cm non-stick loose bottom cake tin
    1 x 900g loaf tin
    12-hole non-stick muffin tray
    1 x 23cm loose-bottomed fluted tart tin
    6 x dariole moulds

- **Baking trays** – Two straightforward baking trays will stand you in good stead. Look for a relatively heavy baking tray, as these won't warp over time.

- **Digital scales** – These are inexpensive, accurate and help reduce washing-up as you can weigh your ingredients directly into the bowl you are mixing in.

- **Silicone moulds** – Some recipes call for silicone moulds of a specific size or shape. They can be a little expensive but are versatile and can be used repeatedly to create interestingly shaped bakes.

INGREDIENTS

- **Eggs** – All the recipes here were written and tested with 'large British eggs'. If you don't know what size of egg you have, you can weigh them into your mixes. You should use approximately 60g per whole egg (cracked), 40g per egg white, and 20g per egg yolk.

- **Butter** – I typically use unsalted butter and add a little salt to my recipes. You can use salted butter, but if so then you might want to omit any additional salt.

- **Sugar** – I like to have five different sugars to hand: caster, granulated, demerara, light brown and dark brown. These bring different flavours and textures to your bakes. If the recipe doesn't specify the type of sugar, then use caster or granulated. Caster has a finer texture than granulated, so it is better at dissolving into batters and mixtures, often making it easier to work with. However, if the ingredients list recommends caster sugar, don't be put off if you only have granulated.

- **Flour** – To create the recipes in this book, you will need three types of flour: plain, self-raising and strong white bread flour. You can make your own self-raising flour by adding 1 teaspoon of baking powder per 100g of plain flour. For a successful bake, you must use the correct type of flour.

- **Milk** – I use whole milk when baking for its added richness. However, you can use whatever is in your fridge for any of the recipes here.

- **Cream** – I always use double cream, rather than single. Double cream can be whipped and hold its shape, whereas single cream lacks the fat content to do this. Alternatively, you can use whipping cream if you prefer.

- **Salt** – If a recipe asks for salt, this relates to basic table salt. Some recipes also have suggestions to use flaky salt, which adds another texture to your bakes. If you don't have flaky salt and want to substitute for table salt, reduce the volume by half (e.g. 1 teaspoon becomes ½ teaspoon).

NOTES ON GLUTEN-FREE BAKING

I have been baking gluten-free for well over 10 years, so my gluten-intolerant brother can eat my bakes. Some of our first attempts were not the best, but we kept practising and testing recipes until we got to the point where I genuinely can't tell the difference between most of the gluten-free and regular versions here.

Some people who bake gluten-free create their own flour blends and alter blends for specific recipes. I admire this work, but this has never appealed to me. I always just wanted to bake. My gluten-free baking is very simple, requires only a few specialist ingredients and typically follows the same techniques as regular baking. I hope that seeing the simplicity of the gluten-free amendments I suggest will help alleviate any concerns you have about baking gluten-free. Part of the reason these recipes work so well with simple modifications is that I have found what bakes naturally lend themselves to gluten-free baking over the years. These are the styles of bakes I am practised in, comfortable with, and am now sharing with you.

HOW TO USE GLUTEN-FREE AMENDMENTS

Throughout, all gluten-containing ingredients will be followed by ingredients or a 'gf' note in brackets. If you are baking gluten-free, substitute the ingredients in the list for the ingredients in brackets. See overleaf for gluten-free ingredient notes.

If baking for someone with an intolerance or allergy to gluten, it is important to check the labels on everything you use. Some ingredients can have gluten-containing ingredients in a particular brand's recipes (e.g. barley in chocolate and cola), so always check the labels and find a brand that doesn't contain gluten.

NOTES ON GLUTEN-FREE INGREDIENTS

- **Flour** – I use premade shop-bought gluten-free plain and self-raising flour blends. They are typically designed to be used as one-to-one replacements for regular wheat flour and they do a great job. The key is to be consistent with the flour blend you use. You will learn how the flour behaves when baking, leading to better results over time. I use the Doves Farm 'Freee' range of gluten-free flours and have done for many years.

- **Plain flour** – In recipes that contain plain flour, a gluten-free plain flour blend is the alternative. Gluten-free flours can sometimes need a little extra liquid compared to other flours when used for pastry or biscuits.

- **Self-raising flour** – Gluten-free self-raising flour blends have the addition of baking powder, as normal, but also often contain some xanthan gum to help bind the bake.

- **Xanthan gum** – This is a stabiliser, thickener and binder. It is added in small quantities to some gluten-free bakes to help prevent them from being overly crumbly. If xanthan gum is needed, it will be listed along with the gluten-free flour and should be added to your mix at the same time as the flour.

- **Psyllium husk powder** – This a specialised ingredient, which you will need to buy online or from health food stores. Only one recipe uses this ingredient, the babas on page 164. Babas are this book's closest cousin to bread, and the psyllium husk powder helps provide structure in the dough as it proves. I discovered the use of psyllium husk powder in Becky Excell's, *How to Make Anything Gluten-Free*. I highly recommend her book for some fantastic savoury recipes (including bread) beyond the sweet recipes in *Peter Bakes*.

- **Baking powder** – Some regular baking powder brands are gluten-free. However, it is important to check the ingredients on the packet you pick up in the shops, as not all baking powders are suitable for gluten-free baking.

NOTES ON HANDY TECHNIQUES

These are just a couple of techniques that are useful to understand beyond the depth that I explain them in the recipes.

How to fill a piping bag

- First, fit the piping bag with a nozzle if using. Cut a small opening at the narrow end of the bag just wide enough to fit half of the nozzle through. Put the nozzle into the bag and pull it out the end. The bag should snuggly fit halfway up the nozzle.

- Open a piping bag and place it into a tall jug or wide glass. Unfold the top of the piping bag and roll it over the edge of the jug.

- Fill the piping bag with your mixture, pressing it into the jug. Lift up the overhanging pieces of the piping bag and pull out of the jug.

- Use your hands to press out any air bubbles from the mixture and move the mixture down towards the bottom of the piping bag. Tie or clip shut the open end of the bag. If not using a nozzle already fitted, use scissors to cut an opening in the bottom of the piping bag.

How to pipe

- Twist the top of the piping bag just above the mixture, so it becomes tight and presses down on the mixture in the bag. Hold the twisted top of the bag in between your thumb and forefinger of your dominant hand, so it is resting on the mixture. Rest your non-dominant hand at the bottom of the bag. Squeeze your dominant hand, from the top of the bag to pipe out the mixture and use your non-dominant hand to guide where the piping bag goes.

- As you pipe out more mixture, the bag will feel less taut. Retwist the top of the bag to create tension again before resuming piping. Try to apply consistent, even pressure to the bag to result in the neatest piping results.

Creaming

- This is the action of beating together butter and sugar, so the sugar mostly dissolves and the mixture traps air and gains volume. This is best done with an electric hand whisk or stand mixer with a paddle attachment. Don't rush the step of creaming butter and sugar when baking cakes. You should beat with an electric mixer for about 3 to 5 minutes to ensure the mixture is very light and airy. Scrape down the sides of the bowl every minute or so to make sure all of the butter and sugar is incorporated.

Folding

- Folding is a way to combine two or more mixtures gently. It is the technique used when we want to avoid deflating a batter that we have incorporated air into (e.g. a Swiss roll batter), or overmixing something that could split (e.g. fillings made with whipped cream). It is best to use a flexible spatula and a large bowl for folding.

- In a single motion, scrape around the outside of half of the bowl, then scrape the spatula down to the bottom of the bowl and lift the batter folding it over itself. Turn the bowl 90 degrees and repeat the process until the mixture is fully combined.

How to line a cake tin

- Use your hands to spread a thin layer of softened butter on the inside of the cake tin around the sides and the base.

- Cut a circle of non-stick baking paper to a little bigger than the size of your tin. This is easiest done by cutting a square of baking paper a little larger than the tin. Fold this in half and then in half again to create a smaller square. Fold this square in half across the closed edge to create a triangle and fold in half along the same edge one or two more times so you have a thin triangle. Lay the triangle over the tin and centre the point in the middle of the tin. Cut the baking paper to size by slicing a rounded cut off the end of the paper where it meets the rim of the tin. Unfold the paper to reveal a circle.

- Place the circle into the base of your greased tin and press out flat with your hands. If it comes a little up the sides of the tin, make sure it is pressed flush into the corners.

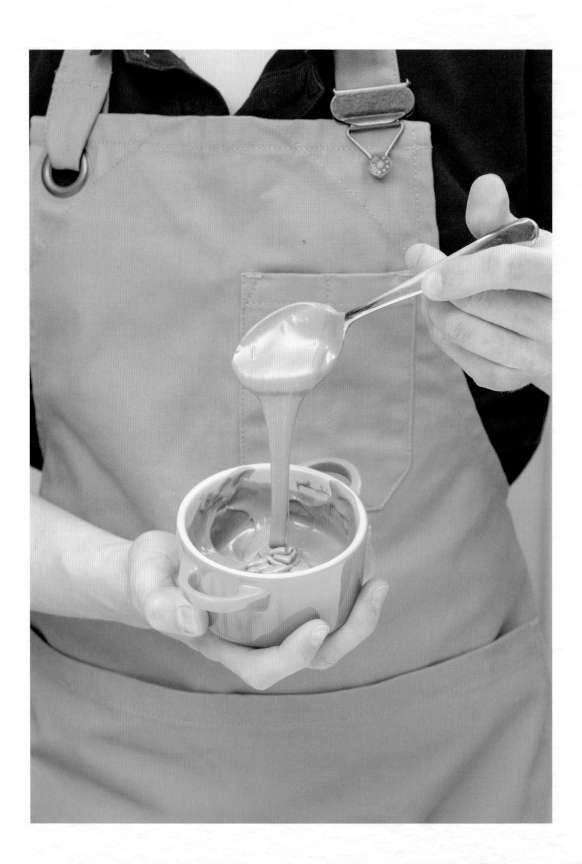

CHAPTER 1
BASICS

These simple recipes are the building blocks for most of the bakes I make, and many later recipes in this book refer back to these for some of their major components. I love creating new recipes or tweaking old favourites with different fillings, toppings or flavours. I hope you can use this chapter as a starting point from which you devise your own recipes, too.

ROUGH PUFF PASTRY

INGREDIENTS

350g plain flour (gf plain
    flour + 1 teaspoon
    xanthan gum)
½ teaspoon salt
50g unsalted butter, chilled
    and cut into small cubes
50g lard, chilled and
    cut into small cubes
    (substitute for butter if you
    prefer)
150ml water
2 teaspoons lemon juice
125g unsalted butter, in a
    frozen block

This is the pastry I typically pick as my go-to flaky pastry over full puff. The process of folding the frozen butter into the dough is called lamination and creates many thin layers of butter and dough in the pastry. When baked, these layers puff up and separate, creating the classic flaky texture. It might feel like a slightly old-fashioned ingredient, but I am a big advocate for the use of lard in rough puff for both sweet and savoury bakes. It aids greatly in developing those highly desirable crisp and flaky results. However, if you omit the lard and use all butter instead, I guarantee that it will still be great. Before you start, remember to put half a block of butter in the freezer. Also allow time for repeated chilling of your dough in the freezer if you can.

This is a recipe where care and attention in how you roll out and layer the dough improves the consistency of the final product. Still, I do believe that the precision required is often over-exaggerated. It's not quite true that any small slip up will ruin the end product, so please don't be put off trying this style of pastry. The simple requirement is for you to create layers of butter and dough. If you achieve any form of layering, no matter how uneven or messy, you will create a flaky result that is buttery and delicious – not to mention wildly impressive to your friends and family!

METHOD

1. Mix the flour and salt in a large bowl and briefly rub in the cubes of chilled butter and lard. Leave lumps of these in the mix. Add the water and the lemon juice and mix until it becomes a rough dough.

2. Roll out this dough on a floured worktop into a long rectangle.

3. Grate a third of the frozen butter over the bottom two-thirds of the dough. Fold the top third over the butter, brush off any excess flour from the top of that portion of dough, then fold the bottom third over the folded top third. Now place the dough and the remaining butter in the freezer for 10 to 15 minutes.

4. Turn the dough 90 degrees and roll out into a long rectangle again.

5. Grate the second third of frozen butter over the bottom two-thirds and repeat the folding process. Place in the freezer for 10 to 15 minutes, then repeat once more.

Tips
- If you are pushed for time, you can complete all of the rolling and folding stages in one without chilling in between.

- Try to keep the edges of the dough as straight as possible while rolling and folding. This will help to keep your layers even. You can use a dough scraper to encourage the sides to be straight.

GF Tips
- When rolling out, the dough can start to fall apart a little more than with regular flour. You just need to be careful when rolling it out. If it starts to break around the edges, use your hands to force it together and continue rolling again. I find you sometimes need a little bit of brute force with GF pastry!

CHOUX PASTRY

INGREDIENTS

Makes about 36 medium-sized buns.

For the choux pastry
50g water
50g milk
40g butter
5g caster sugar
¼ teaspoon salt
70g strong bread flour
(gf self-raising flour +
½ teaspoon xanthan gum)
2 large eggs, beaten

For the craquelin
50g butter, softened
50g demerara sugar
50g plain flour (gf plain
flour)

Choux is my favourite pastry to make. I love getting into the rhythm of piping a large batch of choux, which has to be one of the most satisfying and relaxing aspects of baking. I nearly always recommend baking choux with the addition of craquelin. This adds a delightful, sweet crunch to the end product and controls the choux's growth, so you end up with more consistent shaping. If using craquelin, remember to prepare and freeze it before making the choux dough.

For me, the most important part of making good choux is in the baking. You need to bake it for longer than you might expect. If the choux isn't fully baked or dried out enough inside, it will collapse when cool. Take the choux to quite a dark colour. This will be a good indication that you will have a crisp hollow shell that will hold up once cool.

METHOD

Preheat the oven to 175°C fan/ 185°C conventional/gas mark 4.5. Line 2 baking trays with baking paper.

1. Place the water, milk, butter, sugar and salt in a pan. Place over a medium heat until the butter has melted and the mixture just begins to show the first couple of bubbles.

2. Take off the heat, throw in the flour and beat to combine. Now beat and press this very thick mixture against the side of the pan, over a high heat for 1 to 2 minutes.

3. Transfer the mixture into a stand mixer with a paddle attachment and leave to cool. Once the mixture is barely warm, gradually add the eggs mixing at high speed until a reluctant dropping consistency is reached. It should hold a hanging V shape when dropped off a spatula.

4. To make profiterole shapes, pipe small mounds onto your baking tray (about 2cm to 3cm diameter) with at least 2cm in between them to allow for growth. Wet your finger and press down any 'tails' on top of the mounds. If you want to add craquelin, do it now before you bake your choux without pressing down any tails with a wet finger first.

5. Bake for about 30 to 35 minutes or until very deep brown and drying out inside. A larger shape requires longer baking.

GF Tips
- The method is exactly the same. However, the roux (mixture that is cooked out once the flour has been added) is typically not as smooth as a roux with strong flour. This is to be expected and the end result still turns out very well.

- I also find GF choux doesn't rise quite as evenly as regular choux, so I recommend topping with craquelin to help achieve consistent shaping results.

Make the craquelin
1. Mix the butter with the sugar and flour until fully combined.

2. Use a rolling pin to spread the mix out as thin as you can between 2 sheets of baking paper, and then freeze.

3. Use a cookie cutter to cut the frozen craquelin into circles the same size, or slightly larger than the piped choux. Top each choux mound with a craquelin circle.

4. Bake as instructed above.

SWEET SHORTCRUST PASTRY

INGREDIENTS

Makes enough pastry to line up to a 25cm round tart tin.

200g plain flour (gf plain flour + ½ teaspoon xanthan gum)
100g butter, cold and cubed
½ teaspoon salt
30g icing sugar
1 large egg yolk (reserve the white)
1 tablespoon water
20g cocoa powder (optional – use this to replace 20g of flour if you want to make chocolate pastry)

Shortcrust is simple and plain, but a pastry case is an excellent canvas for creativity and innovation in the kitchen. Most delicious sweet things work very nicely indeed in a pastry case!

If you're making this a full 'glutened' bake, make sure you don't overwork the dough or put in too much water. This will create a tougher end result. We want a short, buttery pastry that is just as enjoyable to eat as the filling. It's an important step to let the pastry rest and chill in the fridge before and after rolling. This allows the flour to hydrate fully, makes the dough easier to handle and prevents it from shrinking back too much when baked.

METHOD

1. Pulse the flour, butter, salt and icing sugar in a food processor until it resembles fine breadcrumbs and no large lumps of butter remain. Alternatively, rub in the butter with your fingertips.

2. Add the egg yolks and water to the food processor and whizz until the mix begins to clump together. Alternatively, mix through the wet ingredients with a table knife until it clumps together. Tip this out onto your surface and lightly work it together to form a smooth dough that isn't sticky.

3. Cover with cling film or baking paper, flatten into a shallow disk and chill in the fridge for at least 30 minutes.

To blind bake your pastry
Preheat the oven to 180°C fan/ 190°C conventional/gas mark 5.

1. On a lightly floured surface, roll out the pastry to about the thickness of a £1 coin. Frequently turn your dough 90 degrees while rolling to ensure it isn't sticking to the surface and to encourage it to stay as round as possible. If the edges begin to crack, press them together or trim them off to prevent further cracking.

2. Gently lay your tart tin on the pastry and cut a circle of pastry about 3.5cm wider than the tin all around.

3. Roll up the pastry back around your rolling pin brushing off any excess flour from underneath as you go.

4. Unroll the pastry from the rolling pin, gently draping it over the tart tin, leaving overhang all the way around.

5. Simultaneously lift the overhanging pastry up with one hand and press it into the corner of the tart tin with the other hand. Do this all the way around. You can use a small piece of excess dough to press the dough tightly into all the edges of the tin.

6. Prick the pastry base all over with a fork. Place back into the fridge to chill for 20 minutes.

7. Line the pastry with a layer of oven-safe cling film or a scrunched and un-scrunched piece of baking paper. Fill this about three-quarters full with baking beans or dried beans to weigh the pastry down.

Continues overleaf . . .

SWEET SHORTCRUST PASTRY
CONTINUED

8. Bake for about 15 minutes. Remove from the oven and take out the lining and weights. Use a sharp knife pressed flat against the tart tin edge to trim away any overhanging pastry. Optionally, lightly brush the inside of the pastry with beaten reserved egg white. This will create a protective barrier for the pastry and keep it crisp when filled.

9. Place the pastry case back in the oven for about 10 minutes or until golden brown all over. If the edges of the tart case are browning too quickly, cover them gently with kitchen foil.

GF Tips

- I find it easier to work with a slightly higher hydration dough when it is gluten-free, so I add 1 to 2 extra teaspoons of water. The dough shouldn't be sticky or wet, but you want quite a pliable texture to aid rolling out and shaping.

- You often have to handle a GF dough more than regular dough. The dough needs to be very well combined not to crack. If it starts to crack excessively when rolling out, often the best course of action is to give it a good knead before rolling out again.

BASIC CAKES

For this chapter I have chosen four basic – but delicious! – cakes. These four basic recipes are both simple and brilliant, because if you can bake them, then you can build on them to create a wide variety of cakes by combining them with different fillings and coverings. All these cakes lend themselves incredibly well to gluten-free baking. If you're new to baking without gluten, cake is definitely the safest and easiest place to start.

BEFORE YOU START . . .
BAKING TIMES

You never want a cake to be dry, so to prevent this, you have to pay attention to the baking time. You can feel blind, having no idea what the cake looks like in its centre, but there are a few ways to check the 'doneness' of a cake. I don't think any single test is best, and I try to recruit as many as possible. They each tell you a little more about the bake and combine to give a good picture of how well your cake is baked.

The Skewer Test
Poke a skewer into the centre of a cake, hold it there for a couple of seconds, then draw it out of the cake. Typically, you want to see the skewer come out clean as this means the cake is baked. If batter is pulled out on the skewer, your cake likely needs more time in the oven.

The Poke Test
Gently pressing on the top of a sponge can give you feedback. If it holds its shape fairly well and springs back to a light touch, it should be baked. You're really testing to see if the cake has structure – which means it is baked – or if it is still just batter and needs more time.

The Shrink Back Test
Most cakes will begin to slightly pull back from the sides of the tin when baking. Slight separation between the tin and cake can be an indication it is baked.

The Listening Test
This test looks funny, but trust me, it works! I have to credit John Whaite from series three of *GBBO* for teaching me this technique! Bring your ear close to the cake and listen. Cake is baked from a loose batter consistency to a solid, so listening to how wet the cake is can tell us a lot. What I listen for is a gentle bubble. If you can't hear anything, that often means it is an overbaked sponge. If it sounds very wet, you know it's underbaked. The more you do this, the more valuable it will be as a technique. Take note of the sound and how that relates to the quality of the final bake and use this to calibrate for the next time you bake.

VICTORIA SPONGE

INGREDIENTS

150g butter, softened
150g caster sugar
150g self-raising flour (gf)
3 large eggs
1½ teaspoons baking
    powder (gf)
1½ teaspoons vanilla extract
    (optional)

I make a Victoria sponge using a cross between the all-in-one and creaming methods. First, I cream the butter and sugar with an electric mixer for a good amount of time – 3 to 5 minutes – to help lighten the sponge. Then I add all the remaining ingredients in one step, which prevents the mixture from curdling, as often happens when adding eggs.

METHOD

Preheat the oven to 160°C fan/ 170°C conventional/gas mark 3.5. Grease and base line 2 x 18cm cake tins.

1. Cream together the butter and sugar with a stand mixer paddle attachment or electric hand whisk until considerably lighter and fluffy (this will take about 5 minutes).

2. Add in the remaining ingredients and mix gently until it just comes together as a smooth mixture.

3. Split the mixture evenly between the 2 tins and bake for 15 to 20 minutes or until a skewer comes out clean and you can hear the cake very gently bubbling.

4. Leave in the tins for about 5 minutes before turning out onto a wire rack to cool.

MADEIRA CAKE

INGREDIENTS

150g butter, softened
150g caster sugar
225g self-raising flour
    (gf + ¼ teaspoon
    xanthan gum)
3 large eggs
2 tablespoons milk
1 lemon, zested

Madeira cake is a slightly firmer cake owing to the ratios in the sponge. But the method used is exactly the same as that for a Victoria sponge . . . so, once you've mastered one, you've mastered them both.

I recommend the following baking times: 18cm round and 20cm square: 30 to 35 minutes; loaf tin: 40 to 45 minutes.

METHOD

Preheat the oven to 160°C fan/ 170°C conventional/gas mark 3.5. Grease and base line an 18cm round cake tin, 20cm square tin or a 900g loaf tin.

1. Cream together the butter and sugar with a stand mixer paddle attachment or electric hand whisk until considerably lighter and fluffy (this will take 3 to 5 minutes).

2. Add the remaining ingredients and stir through until combined.

3. Add into your tin, level off and bake for the times directed above and a skewer comes out clean and it is evenly golden on top.

4. Leave in the tin for about 5 minutes before turning out onto a wire rack to cool.

GENOISE SPONGE

INGREDIENTS

3 large eggs
100g caster sugar
100g self-raising flour (gf)
35g butter, melted and
    cooled

Genoise is a beautifully light and soft cake. The critical point in the technique is in folding in the flour and butter. As soon as you can no longer see clumps of flour or streaks of butter, stop folding – if you carry on that will continue to deflate the batter and result in a dense sponge. Don't worry about making this, though. Be confident with your movements and the result will turn out well.

METHOD

Preheat the oven to 160°C fan/ 170°C conventional/gas mark 3.5. Grease and base line a deep 20cm cake tin.

The first step can be done one of two ways.

1. Place the eggs and sugar in a bowl set over a pan of barely simmering water. (Make sure the bowl isn't touching the water.) Whisk – a manual whisk is fine, but you will find this easiest with an electric hand whisk – for about 5 minutes, at which point the mixture will be very thick and pale, 2 to 3 times the original volume, and will hold a strong ribbon trail.

   OR

2. Whisk the eggs and sugar on full speed with an electric hand whisk or stand mixer until you achieve the thick, pale texture described above.

To complete the sponge

1. Sieve over the flour and gently fold in using a flexible spatula. Once the flour is almost fully incorporated, pour in the butter around the side of the bowl and fold in until just combined. Remember – be careful not to fold the batter too much at this stage.

2. Gently pour the mixture into your prepared tin and bake for about 25 minutes or until a skewer comes out clean and you can hear a gentle foamy bubble.

3. Cool in the tin for about 5 minutes, then turn out onto a wire rack to cool fully.

SWISS ROLL SPONGE

INGREDIENTS

4 large eggs
110g caster sugar
1 teaspoon vanilla bean
    paste
110g self-raising flour (gf)

This type of cake is called a 'fatless sponge' as it contains no butter or oil. With its very short bake time, it's one of the fastest cakes you can whip together. Plus, you can use it for much more than Swiss rolls. It's perfect for ice cream cakes, mousse cakes and more!

If you are making a Swiss roll with the sponge, make sure you don't overbake it, as this is one of the main reasons for a Swiss roll cracking. It should sound quite actively bubbly but still pass the skewer test.

METHOD

Preheat the oven to 170°C fan/ 180°C conventional/gas mark 4.

Grease and line a 33cm x 23cm Swiss roll tin with non-stick baking paper making sure the paper is tightly tucked into the corners of the tin. If you don't have a Swiss roll tin, you can always use a roasting tin.

1. In a stand mixer or using an electric hand mixer, whisk the eggs with the sugar and vanilla until they reach ribbon stage. The batter should be very thick, pale, doubled in size and you should be able to write a figure of 8 with it before the mixture sinks back in.

2. Sieve the flour over the mix and gently fold in using a flexible spatula. Once there are no more pockets of flour, pour into the prepared tin and bake in the oven for 8 to 10 minutes or until it's lightly golden and sounds quite actively bubbly.

3. If turning into a Swiss roll, while the cake is in the oven, cover a sheet of baking paper slightly larger than the cake with a sprinkling of caster sugar.

4. Once the sponge is baked, leave it to cool for 3 to 5 minutes in the tin. Then turn out the sponge onto the sugar-covered baking paper. Peel off the top baking paper from the sponge, then rest it back on. Use the bottom baking paper to roll the sponge into a tight spiral, then unroll and leave to cool between the double layer of baking paper.

MERINGUES

It's really valuable to understand the three main methods of making meringue. They each result in a meringue with different qualities, which lends itself to different bakes. You will have leftover yolks when making meringue. Curd (see page 41), or crème pat (see page 46), are great ways to use these up and are terrific accompaniments for meringue.

FRENCH MERINGUE

INGREDIENTS

3 large egg whites
150g caster sugar
50g icing sugar

This is also called a 'cold meringue' as the egg whites are not heated in the process. Be sure to bake the meringue quite quickly after mixing because it will begin to weep and lose volume after about 10 to 15 minutes.

METHOD

1. Use an electric hand whisk or stand mixer at full speed to whisk the egg whites to a frothy cloud-like consistency.

2. Gradually add the caster sugar, about a tablespoon at a time, mixing at medium speed. Wait about 15 seconds between each addition.

3. Once all the caster sugar has been added, continue whisking at medium speed until the mixture no longer feels gritty between your fingers. Then whisk in the icing sugar at low speed until combined. The meringue should be smooth and glossy.

To bake small meringue kisses
Preheat the oven to 100°C fan/110°C conventional/gas mark ¼. Line 2 baking trays.

1. Vertically pipe small peaks of meringue from a piping bag with a 1–1.5cm round hole onto the baking trays. Bake for about 45 minutes, until they can be gently peeled away from the baking paper without breaking apart.

ITALIAN MERINGUE

INGREDIENTS

240g sugar
40ml water
3 large egg whites

This is a stable meringue made by whisking egg whites with a hot sugar syrup that will hold its shape for a long time without baking. Keep whisking the meringue until cold to ensure it stays glossy and firm long after it's made. Italian meringue is perfect to use as a cake covering or for piping onto bakes as a finishing touch.

METHOD

1. Put the sugar into a pan with the water. Place over a high heat, stirring all the time until the sugar has dissolved and it begins to boil. Stop stirring and leave on the heat to boil.

2. While the sugar is on the heat, whisk the egg whites in a stand mixer until they look like frothy clouds, then turn down the speed of the mixer to low.

3. Take the temperature of the sugar syrup. Once it reaches 121°C, take it off the heat and slowly stream it into the egg whites down the side of the bowl, while whisking at high speed.

4. Continue whisking until the meringue has fully cooled to room temperature and is firm and glossy.

SWISS MERINGUE

INGREDIENTS

3 large egg whites
200g sugar

Swiss meringue is another stable meringue that can be eaten without further baking. This results in a slightly fluffier texture than Italian meringue and has similar uses to its Italian counterpart.

METHOD

1. Place the egg whites and sugar in a large mixing bowl or the bowl of a stand mixer over a pan of gently simmering water. Stir until the sugar has dissolved and it doesn't feel gritty when pinched between your fingers. Continue heating the meringue until the temperature reads between 70 and 80°C.

2. Remove the bowl from the heat and place into a stand mixer. Whisk at medium-speed until cooled to room temperature, glossy and stiff.

BUTTERCREAMS

Buttercreams are fantastic to use for a clean coating on cakes. But still I try to use buttercream quite sparingly as it can make a bake too sweet and sickly. They are best eaten when soft at room temperature. They simply aren't as enjoyable to eat when cold and their high butter content means they firm up and go quite solid in the fridge.

ITALIAN MERINGUE BUTTERCREAM

SWISS MERINGUE BUTTERCREAM

ITALIAN MERINGUE BUTTERCREAM

INGREDIENTS

1 quantity Italian meringue (page 27)
210g unsalted butter, softened
½ teaspoon salt
2 teaspoons vanilla bean paste (optional)

SWISS MERINGUE BUTTERCREAM

INGREDIENTS

1 quantity Swiss meringue (page 27)
200g unsalted butter, softened
½ teaspoon salt
2 teaspoons vanilla bean paste

This is my go-to buttercream. If you have a stand mixer, it is effortless to make. It takes a lot of mixing to get a smooth glossy meringue and creamy buttercream, which means you will really get your money's worth from the machine. If at any point the buttercream appears split or soupy, don't worry; just continue mixing at high speed and the buttercream should come together again.

METHOD

1. Make your quantity of Italian meringue and whisk until cooled.

2. Whisk the butter in a separate bowl with the salt until light and smooth. Gradually add this to the meringue a heaped dessert spoon at a time, beating at medium high speed with a paddle attachment between additions. Continue adding butter and beating until the buttercream is smooth, has thickened and holds its shape.

3. Mix through the vanilla, or other flavouring.

This buttercream is very similar to an Italian meringue buttercream. It is very light, smooth and stable, which makes it perfect for covering layer cakes. These buttercreams also take on flavour incredibly well. You might like to whisk through about 100g to 200g of ganache or a thick fruit purée once you have finished mixing the buttercream.

METHOD

1. Make your quantity of Swiss meringue and whisk until cooled.

2. Whisk the butter in a separate bowl with the salt until light and smooth. Gradually add this to the meringue a heaped dessert spoon at a time, beating at medium high speed with a paddle attachment between additions. Continue adding butter and beating until the buttercream is smooth, has thickened and holds its shape.

3. Mix through the vanilla paste or other flavouring.

CRÈME AU BEURRE

AMERICAN STYLE BUTTERCREAM

CRÈME AU BEURRE

INGREDIENTS

100g caster sugar
1 tablespoon water
3 large egg yolks
100g butter, softened
½ teaspoon salt
2 teaspoons vanilla bean
    paste (optional)

AMERICAN STYLE
BUTTERCREAM

INGREDIENTS

250g butter, softened
½ teaspoon salt
500g icing sugar
3 tablespoons milk
2 teaspoons vanilla bean
    paste (optional)

This is almost the reverse of an Italian meringue buttercream. The process is very similar; however, you use egg yolks instead of the whites. Because you are using the yolks, this is a very rich buttercream so think about pairing it with bitter or sharp flavours through the rest of the bake. It also turns out more yellow in colour, which is good to know if you plan to cover a cake with the icing.

My mum used to make this type of buttercream for birthday cakes when we were younger. I must admit that nowadays this isn't my favourite buttercream because it is so sweet. However, it is perfect for making a nostalgic cupcake or birthday cake!

For light, smooth buttercream, it's key to cream the butter and sugar at high speed for a long time. Don't rush this step.

METHOD

1. Stir together the sugar and water in a pan over a high heat until dissolved. Stop stirring and leave it to boil; it needs to reach between 118°C and 121°C on a sugar thermometer.

2. Place the egg yolks in the bowl of a stand mixer and whisk on medium speed while gradually streaming in the hot sugar syrup. Whisk at high speed until the mixture has cooled down.

3. Whisk the butter in a separate bowl with the salt until light and smooth. Gradually add this to the egg yolks a heaped dessert spoon at a time, beating at medium high speed with a paddle attachment between additions. Continue adding butter and beating until the buttercream is smooth, has thickened and holds its shape.

4. Mix through the vanilla or other flavouring.

METHOD

1. Cream the butter and salt together in a bowl. Then, sieve over the icing sugar about 50g at a time, creaming the mixture at high speed for about 1 minute after each addition. The buttercream should be very light and smooth.

2. After the sugar, add the milk 1 tablespoon at a time to loosen to a softly spreadable texture that still holds its shape. You might not need to use all the milk.

3. Mix through the vanilla paste, or other flavouring of your choice.

GANACHE

INGREDIENTS

Dark chocolate ganache
200g double cream
150g dark chocolate

Milk chocolate ganache
200g double cream
200g milk chocolate

**White chocolate
 ganache**
200g double cream
300g white chocolate

Ganache is wildly simple to make – it needs only two ingredients and there's just one step to follow. The texture of the final product depends on:

1. The temperature of the ganache. A colder ganache will be firmer. A warmer ganache will be softer.

2. The ratio of the cream to chocolate. A higher proportion of cream results in a softer ganache; a higher proportion of chocolate results in a firmer ganache.

3. The type of chocolate used. Chocolate with a higher cocoa solids percentage (i.e. dark chocolate) will set up firmer. This is why I have given different ratios for dark, milk and white chocolate ganache here.

You may find that these ratios aren't quite right for the type of chocolate you use or the texture you like. Feel free to change these ratios as you wish. It's also good to remember that this isn't a recipe that requires precise measurement and the window of ratios that you can use is very wide.

METHOD

1. Heat the cream until it just begins to bubble. Remove from the heat and add the chocolate, broken into chunks. Allow it to sit for about a minute before gently stirring from the centre out until all the chocolate has melted and the ganache is one smooth, glossy colour and texture.

USES

Whipped ganache
1. Leave the ganache to cool to room temperature; it should be noticeably thicker.

2. Beat the mixture with an electric hand whisk until lightened in colour and texture. Do not over whip as this can cause it to separate.

3. This ganache can be piped onto cakes and cupcakes.

Cake covering
1. Leave the ganache to cool to room temperature. It should be a spreadable consistency for icing cakes.

2. If it's too loose to spread, place in the fridge for 15 minutes or so to firm up. If too firm, place the bowl over a pan of simmering water for about 30 seconds, then gently stir together.

Truffles
1. Leave the ganache to cool and set in the fridge for a couple of hours.

2. Take a teaspoon of the mixture, roll into a ball and cover in cocoa powder.

Glaze
1. Allow the ganache to cool to a thick fluid consistency (i.e. it is still warm). Pour over a cake and then chill to create a simple glaze.

CARAMELISED WHITE CHOCOLATE

200 to 500g white
chocolate

This is one of those magical baking processes. Baking white chocolate in the oven feels like it should be wrong, but trust the process: it works! Some people find white chocolate quite boring and single toned, but this method gives rise to lots of roasted caramel notes that create a brand-new flavour profile for you to use in your baking.

I recommend using the caramelised white chocolate straight away or setting it in small silicone moulds if you want to use it later. The chocolate will set firm at room temperature or in the fridge.

METHOD

Preheat the oven to 120°C fan/ 130°C conventional/gas mark 2.

1. Spread the white chocolate out in an even layer on a rimmed baking tray or roasting tin. Place in the oven for 10 minutes.

2. Remove from the oven and mix with a spatula or wooden spoon until very smooth. The chocolate will look grainy when you first start stirring; keep vigorously mixing and it will become smooth again.

3. Place the chocolate back in the oven for a further 10 minutes, remove and stir until smooth again. Repeat this process 3 or 4 more times until it takes on a beautiful dark caramel colour.

CARAMEL

Many people are scared of making caramel – and are worried about the mixture crystallising – but knowledge of just a few rules makes it a far less daunting task. There are two types of caramel – dry and wet.

A dry caramel (made without water) will not crystallise; the only danger is that you might create an uneven caramel. Cooking a dry caramel over a lower heat for a longer time will help create a more even caramel.

A wet caramel – which uses sugar and water – typically makes a more evenly coloured caramel; however, it is at risk of crystallising.

If you follow these two rules, your wet caramel will not crystallise:

1. Do NOT use a non-stick pan.

2. Once the sugar has all dissolved and it starts to boil, do NOT stir the caramel.

The final rule with caramel is to be brave and confident. You want a dark caramel colour that brings amazing roasty, toasty caramelised flavours. You might burn a couple of caramels as you start out, as it can turn from a beautiful caramel to burned in a short time, but with experience you will get better at judging the point to take it off the heat.

Caramel is also surprisingly easy to wash up. Just fill the pan with water and bring it to a boil. This will clean the sugar off the pan and make it very easy to wipe out.

WET CARAMEL

INGREDIENTS

200g sugar
3 tablespoons water

METHOD

1. Mix your sugar and water together in a pan over high heat. Remember: do not use a non-stick pan!

2. Continue stirring until all the sugar has dissolved and the mixture begins to boil. At this point, stop stirring and remove the spoon from the pan.

3. The syrup will stop rapidly boiling and will begin to develop an amber colour. If it is colouring unevenly, you can give the pan a gentle swirl, but do not stir the mixture.

4. Once you are happy that it has reached a deep caramel colour remove the pan from the heat and use the caramel for whatever purpose is planned.

DRY CARAMEL

INGREDIENTS

200g sugar

METHOD

1. Place the sugar in a pan over medium heat.

2. Once you can see parts of the sugar melting, give the mixture a stir to encourage it to melt evenly.

3. There will be lumps of sugar forming in the pan; this is okay. Just keep stirring the mixture, breaking up the large lumps and encouraging it all to melt simultaneously.

4. The sugar will begin to take on a caramel colour. Continue stirring until you are happy that all the sugar has taken on an even caramel colour that you're happy to use.

CARAMEL SAUCE

INGREDIENTS

200g sugar
3 tablespoons water
130g double cream (plus or minus 30g depending on the consistency you'd like)
70g butter, cubed (plus or minus 30g depending on the consistency you'd like)
Flaky sea salt (optional)

Caramel sauce will firm up as it chills. If you want a runny consistency once it cools, then remove some butter from the recipe and add additional cream. Likewise, you can add additional butter and reduce the quantity of cream if you want it very firm. To make salted caramel add in some salt, once cooled, tasting as you go.

METHOD

1. Make a wet caramel (page 33) with the sugar and water, taking it to a deep amber.

2. Leave the mixture on the heat and gradually stir in the cream. Be careful: the mixture may spit as it bubbles up.

3. Remove from the heat, leave to cool for a couple of minutes then add in the butter, stirring until combined. Once the mixture is smooth, stir through the salt if desired.

PRALINE

300g blanched nuts
200g sugar
3 tablespoons water
1 teaspoon flaky salt
    (optional)

Praline is a delicious combination of nuts and caramel. Typically, it is made with hazelnuts or almonds, but you can use whatever nut you like; seeds can be very tasty too.

I share three uses for praline here. The first leaves it to set as a crunchy brittle, which adds great flavour and texture to desserts when broken up. The second is to create a praline crumb, which is excellent for finishing bakes with subtle decoration and more caramelly flavours. The third is to turn your praline into a paste. This forms the base for the filling of lots of classic French patisserie. Some nuts don't blend well into a praline paste and stay too thick. Almonds and hazelnuts work well; peanuts make a very, very thick paste; walnuts and pecans do not work! I haven't tried any other varieties, but could be worth an experiment if you fancy testing something new.

METHOD

Preheat your oven to 170°C fan/ 180°C conventional/gas mark 4. Line a baking sheet with a silicone mat or baking paper.

1. Put the nuts on a baking tray and roast in the oven for about 10 minutes, or until they turn slightly darker and release a strong nutty smell into your kitchen.

2. Make a wet caramel with the sugar and water and take it to medium-dark amber (page 33).

3. While the pan is on the heat, throw in the roasted nuts, ideally still warm from roasting. Stir the nuts through the caramel until evenly coated, add the salt if desired and turn out onto your lined baking sheet. Leave at room temperature to cool and set. What you have now is essentially a nut brittle.

4. To make a praline crumb, break up the brittle into smaller pieces and add to a food processor. Whizz the praline until it is broken into smaller pieces and resembles crumbs.

5. To make a praline paste, simply continue blitzing the praline crumb (from almonds or hazelnuts) in the food processor for 5 minutes periodically scraping down the sides of the machine and giving the machine a little time to cool down. The nuts will release their oils and result in a paste.

CRYSTALLISED NUTS

INGREDIENTS

2 teaspoons water
70g sugar
100g nuts

The aim when crystallising nuts is to make a 'bad' caramel that crystallises around the nuts. This results in a very beautiful yet easy to achieve decoration for many bakes. My personal favourite nut to use for this is the pistachio. The coating is near sparkly. It makes for a striking and incredibly appealing decoration when paired with pistachio's green and purple hues. I also prefer to not use blanched nuts for this as I think the colours from the skins of nuts add to this as a decoration.

METHOD

1. Place the water and sugar in a pan over high heat, stirring until it reaches a boil.

2. Once it is bubbling away, throw in the nuts and continue stirring, encouraging the sugar to crystallise. Keep stirring over a high heat until the water has evaporated and the nuts have a snowy-looking coating of sugar around them.

3. Turn out onto a baking sheet lined with baking paper or a silicone mat and leave to cool.

4. These can be left whole, roughly chopped or blitzed into a crumb.

NOUGATINE

INGREDIENTS

250g flaked almonds
400g sugar
100g glucose syrup (can
    substitute for golden
    syrup)
4 tablespoons water
25g butter

Nougatine is a challenging thing to make. You have to work fast and be confident in your movements to get a good result. But done well it is beautiful as structural support for towering desserts like a croquembouche and as decorative shapes for smaller bakes.

You need two specialist pieces of kit to successfully make this, sugar gloves for safety and a large silicone pastry mat for working and rolling out the nougatine.

METHOD

1. Toast the flaked almonds on a baking tray at 150°C fan/160°C conventional/gas mark 3 for about 10 minutes. Once they are golden and toasty, turn off the oven and leave the almonds in to stay warm.

2. Stir together the sugar, glucose and water in a large pan over a high heat; you can continue stirring this mixture while it boils as the glucose syrup prevents it from crystallising. Once it has reached a medium amber or registers 170–175°C, stir through the warm almonds and butter.

3. Pour this out onto a large silicone mat, leave to stand for a couple of minutes. While wearing sugar work gloves, use the silicone mat to lift up one side of the nougatine and press it onto itself. Do this many times all around the nougatine, like you are kneading it. As it cools it will stop sticking to the mat and will come together in a cohesive mass.

4. Once you feel the nougatine is no longer fluid but is cooling down and becoming malleable, it is time to roll it out. Use a heavy rolling pin to roll out the nougatine to about ½ cm thick. If the rolling pin gets stuck, you can lightly oil it to prevent this. Once the nougatine is rolled out, it is ready to shape as you need.

5. You need to roll and shape nougatine while it is warm. If it ever gets too hard to work with, place it back in the oven at about 150°C for 3 to 5 minutes. It should soften down a little and be workable again.

6. You can cut shapes from nougatine using a cookie cutter or knife. You can also mould the nougatine around the outside of a lightly oiled form.

FRUIT PURÉES

INGREDIENTS

250g fruit (frozen or fresh)
25g caster sugar

Fruit purées provide the base flavour for many of my bakes. A more intense flavour and thicker texture comes from simmering the fruit for longer. You can make purées with any type of berry, with mangos, pears, pineapples, plums, nectarines and many more fruits.

METHOD

1. Peel and chop the fruit into a small dice. This isn't necessary for berries, but you will need to chop up the likes of mango, pineapple, apple or pear.

2. Put the sugar and fruit into a pan and bring it to a simmer over a medium heat.

3. Simmer for about 2 minutes for a thin purée, 5 minutes for a medium thickness purée and 7 to 10 minutes for a thick purée. Make sure to stir frequently to avoid it burning to the pan.

4. Whizz the purée with a stick blender and pass through a sieve before chilling.

FRUIT CURDS

Using shop-bought curds in your bakes is super quick and easy – and often very useful. However, if you have the time to make your own, you will thank yourself later, as the flavour of a fresh homemade curd is unbeatable. Making your own also means you can amend the texture or sweetness of the curd as you wish. More butter will make for a thicker curd once cooled, and so will an extra egg yolk. Feel free to add an extra yolk if you want a super thick end product and play about with the quantity of butter, depending on how creamy and thick you like a curd to be.

Avoid boiling the mixture as this will scramble the yolks, but if it does become slightly lumpy at any point, take it off the heat, pass through a sieve and add in your butter straight away. This can help to cool down the curd and prevent it from scrambling any further.

All sorts of fruits work well in curds, so be adventurous! If something sounds delicious, then why not try it?

CURDS FROM FRUIT JUICE

INGREDIENTS

90ml fruit juice (typically citrus fruit)
Zest of your juiced fruit
100g caster sugar
4 large egg yolks
50 to 90g unsalted butter, cubed

METHOD

1. Heat the juice and zest in a non-stick pan to a simmer.

2. Whisk the sugar with the egg yolks in a bowl. Slowly pour in the hot juice while whisking.

3. Return this mixture to the pan and constantly stir over a low heat until thickened – this will take up to 5 to 10 minutes – making sure it doesn't boil. It should thickly coat the back of a spoon. You can also check the temperature to see if it is ready; it should be between 75°C and 82°C.

4. Take the curd off the heat, allow it to cool for a couple of minutes, then add in the butter a couple of cubes at a time while the curd is still warm, whisking to incorporate.

5. Store the curd in an airtight container in the fridge.

CURDS FROM FRUIT PURÉE

INGREDIENTS

175g fruit purée, medium thickness (page 40)
50g caster sugar
3 large egg yolks
40 to 80g unsalted butter, cubed

METHOD

1. Heat the fruit purée in a non-stick pan to a simmer.

2. For steps 2 to 5, use the same method as Curds from Fruit Juice (see above).

QUICK JAM

INGREDIENTS

250g soft fruit, roughly
    chopped
250g jam sugar

It is surprisingly quick and easy to make a simple jam. Jam sugar has added pectin, which makes the mixture set when cool. The basic formula for a jam is one part fruit to one part jam sugar, but you can always jazz up the flavour by adding a little extra something to the mix. For example, you could add rosewater to a raspberry jam, some black pepper to a strawberry jam, or some ground ginger to a rhubarb jam.

METHOD

1. Put the fruit and sugar in a non-stick pan and bring to a boil.

2. Reduce the temperature and simmer for about 4 to 5 minutes.

3. Once the mixture reads 105°C on a sugar thermometer, leave it to cool down to room temperature, then chill in the fridge to set up.

CHANTILLY CREAM

INGREDIENTS

20g icing sugar
2 teaspoons vanilla bean
    paste
200ml double cream

Don't be alarmed . . . Chantilly cream is simply whipped cream with a slightly fancier name! It takes 2 minutes to whip by hand, making it probably the fastest cake filling possible. It's easy to overwhip cream when at firm peaks, so be careful not to over mix it at this stage, or it will become lumpy. If this happens, keep whisking, and you will have butter (solids) and buttermilk (liquids). This is why I think it's best to whip by hand or switch from a machine to whisking by hand once at soft peaks. My favourite texture of Chantilly is to use it when it is at what I call medium-firm peaks. At this stage it can be used to spread onto cakes and it holds its shape without running the risk of overwhipping and going grainy while working with it.

METHOD

1. Add the sugar and vanilla to the cream and whisk to your desired texture.

2. Typically, you are aiming for soft peaks, medium-firm or firm peaks. Soft peaks have some volume but are soft, so won't stand up against gravity. Medium-firm peaks will hold shape and be spreadable but can fall easily from an upturned spatula. Firm peaks will hold their shape when spread and piped and will cling onto an upturned spatula.

CUSTARD

INGREDIENTS

500ml whole milk
3 large egg yolks
50g caster sugar
2 teaspoons vanilla bean
    paste
1 tablespoon cornflour

Making your own custard is very simple, and it tastes so good! Unlike crème Anglaise, this custard recipe contains cornflour. The cornflour does two things. Firstly, it thickens the custard. Second, it stabilises the mixture and prevents the eggs from scrambling. Cornflour thickens the mixture at boiling point, so you want to bring this mixture to the boil stirring all the time. On the other hand, boiling like this would ruin a crème Anglaise.

METHOD

1. Heat the milk in a non-stick pan. Bring this to a simmer.

2. Meanwhile, whisk together the egg yolks, sugar and vanilla until a pale colour, then whisk through the cornflour.

3. Once the milk has come to a simmer, slowly pour it over the egg yolk mix, whisking all the time.

4. Return this mix to the pan and place it over a high heat. Whisk constantly until the mixture begins to boil and thicken.

5. Use straight away or cover the surface directly with cling film or baking paper to prevent a skin from forming.

CRÈME ANGLAISE

INGREDIENTS

150ml whole milk
100ml double cream
3 large egg yolks
40g caster sugar
1 teaspoon vanilla bean
    paste

Its lack of cornflour makes crème Anglaise different from custard, and so the only thickening agent in crème Anglaise is the egg yolk. Without cornflour, the mixture can split and scramble if taken up to too hot a temperature. The yolks will cook and make the mixture thicken at around 80°C. Above this temperature the mixture will start to split. To check if your crème Anglaise is cooked, you can either test the temperature – which should lie between 75°C and 82°C – or assess the thickness by eye. To test the consistency, run your finger through the back of a spoon covered in the crème anglaise: it should hold a strong line.

METHOD

1. Heat the milk and cream in a non-stick pan. Bring this to a simmer.

2. Meanwhile, whisk together the egg yolks, sugar and vanilla until a pale colour.

3. Once the milk and cream has come to a simmer, slowly pour it over the egg yolk mix, whisking all the time. Return this to the pan and place it over a low heat.

4. Stir the mixture over this low heat for about 5 minutes. Do not let it boil as the eggs will scramble and it will become lumpy. The bubbles on the surface should begin to disappear, and the custard will thicken to coat the back of a spoon. Once this happens and you are happy with the thickness, use it straight away or cover the surface with cling film or baking paper to prevent a skin forming.

5. If reheating, do this gently in a pan. Not in the microwave!

CRÈME PÂTISSIÈRE

INGREDIENTS

200ml whole milk
2 large egg yolks
50g caster sugar
15g cornflour
2 teaspoons vanilla bean
    paste
10g butter (optional)

Crème pâtissière forms the base for many classic fillings and toppings, making it an incredibly useful filling to have in your repertoire. Crème pat is extremely versatile, and you can easily adjust the recipe to alter consistency or flavour.

Consistency/texture

This recipe creates a crème pat that sets firm in the fridge and is perfect to use in fillings that require structure (e.g. mille feuille, choux buns, cake fillings). The addition of butter creates a firmer set when cold, which is useful if you want to make a crème pat that slices cleanly. The texture can be altered by increasing or decreasing the quantity of cornflour in the recipe. If your end product is too thick, you can gradually whisk in some milk until you reach your desired texture.

Flavours

There are several ways you can introduce a new flavour to a crème pat. Switch out all or a portion of the milk for a different liquid. Fruit purées, flavoured milks, milk alternatives, liqueurs (not as the majority of the total liquid) and extracts (a few teaspoons) all produce an excellent result. To make a chocolate crème pat, you can substitute half of the cornflour for cocoa powder and switch the butter for chocolate.

METHOD

1. Heat the milk in a non-stick pan and bring to a boil.

2. Meanwhile, whisk the egg yolks with the sugar until slightly lightened in colour. Then whisk through the cornflour and vanilla.

3. Once the milk has come to the boil, slowly pour it into the egg mixture, whisking constantly. Pour this back into the pan and stir vigorously over a high heat until the mixture boils and thickens.

4. Take the crème pat off the heat and stir through the butter (if desired). If there are any lumps in the custard, pass it through a sieve before chilling.

5. Pour into a dish and cover with cling film or baking paper directly over the surface to prevent a skin from forming. It will firm up when chilled in the fridge.

CRÈME LÉGÈRE

INGREDIENTS

1 quantity crème pâtissière
200ml double cream
20g icing sugar

This is my favourite use of crème pat. Crème légère is simply crème pat that is lightened by folding through whipped cream. The result is smoother, lighter and simultaneously creamier than crème pat alone, and is also more stable than whipped cream by itself. It is easier to flavour a crème pat than whipped cream, making it an excellent way to introduce different tastes into fillings.

METHOD

1. Whisk the crème pat to smooth it out. You may wish to pass it through a sieve if there are any lumps.

2. Whisk together the double cream and icing sugar to firm peaks.

3. Fold the double cream through the crème pat until fully combined. Cover and store in the fridge until you're ready to use it.

CRÈME MOUSSELINE

INGREDIENTS

1 quantity crème pâtissière, at room temperature
50g butter, very soft

Crème mousseline is rich, creamy and indulgent. The result is somewhere between a very rich crème pat and a soft, smooth buttercream. Ideally, the crème pat should be around room temperature, not fridge cold, when combining with the butter. This should help with combining the two components smoothly.

METHOD

1. Whisk the crème pat to smooth it out. You may wish to pass it through a sieve if there are any lumps.

2. Whisk the softened butter for a few minutes until considerably lightened in colour and texture.

3. Whisk the butter into the crème pat, adding the butter a heaped dessert spoon at a time until fully combined

OATY CRUMBLE

INGREDIENTS

60g butter
60g demerara sugar
50g pinhead oatmeal
   (substitute for additional
   gf oats)
100g rolled oats (gf oats)
1 pinch of flaky sea salt

I make these golden sweet oats all the time. They are an effortless way to add texture to a bake and create dynamic contrast. Top any creamy, smooth bake with some of these, and it will change the game.

METHOD

Preheat the oven to 180°C fan/ 190°C conventional/gas mark 5. Line a rimmed baking tray with baking paper.

1. Melt the butter in a pan, stir through the demerara sugar, oatmeal, rolled oats and salt.

2. Turn this mixture out onto your prepared baking tray and toast in the oven for about 20 minutes or until deeply golden and toasty, stirring at halfway.

CANDIED PEEL

INGREDIENTS

2 citrus fruits
100g sugar (plus extra for
   dusting)
200ml water

My absolute favourite way to decorate baking is to keep it natural and showcase the ingredients' beauty. Candied peel relies on and celebrates the natural beauty of the fruits used. When you make candied peel, be sure to reserve the syrup that is drained off. This carries a great deal of flavour and is perfect for brushing over sponges or glazing fruits to decorate cakes. Any citrus fruit works brilliantly for this.

METHOD

Heat the oven to 100°C fan/ 110°C conventional/gas mark ¼. Line a baking tray with non-stick paper.

1. Use a vegetable peeler to peel the zest from the citrus fruits.

2. Bring the sugar and water up to a boil in a pan while stirring.

3. Reduce the syrup to a simmer and add in the peel for 10 minutes. Drain the peel, keeping the syrup if you choose.

4. Place the drained peel on a baking sheet and dry out in the oven for about 40 minutes.

5. Remove from the oven, then while still warm, roll your peel in some additional sugar.

ICE CREAM AND SORBET

Ice cream is my favourite sweet treat, so I had to include a couple of recipes here. I got an ice cream machine for my 14th birthday – and I've been making ice cream ever since. Fresh homemade ice cream is excellent! I'm not an ice cream master, but I've included the simple recipes that I use to whip up a fresh batch at home. There are two ice cream base recipes, plus a guide to making sorbet from fruit purée, in this section. There are also ideas to make different flavours from the same base recipe on pages 54 and 55.

METHOD

1. Make the ice cream or sorbet base (see page 51) and chill until fridge cold.

2. Churn in an ice cream machine as per the instructions until a soft-serve consistency is achieved. If you want to add any mix-ins, do this once the ice cream has reached soft-serve consistency and briefly mix until the add-ins are evenly suspended. It is best to pre-chill your mix-ins in the fridge or freezer before mixing them through.

3. Tightly pack into a tub, cover the surface with baking paper followed by the lid and freeze.

CHURNING WITHOUT AN ICE CREAM MACHINE

Using an ice cream machine is the best and easiest way to get great results every time, but you can still make homemade ice cream without a machine. I list two different methods here.

Food processor churning

1. Freeze your ice cream base in a wide tray, so it is fully frozen and solid.

2. Break the frozen base up into small pieces and add to a food processor. Blitz until smooth. Add this smooth mixture into a tub, cover and freeze again until scoopable.

Freeze and stir

1. Pour the ice cream base into a bowl and freeze for 30 to 45 minutes; the edges should begin to freeze. Pull it from the freezer and stir or whisk the ice cream to make sure it is chilling evenly.

2. Repeat the freezing and stirring process as the ice cream is chilling and thickening until the ice cream is a thick, soft-serve consistency. This should take 5 or 6 turns.

3. The more frequently you stir the ice cream, the smoother the result will be. If you leave it for too long between stirs, it can become lumpy and icy.

CUSTARD BASE ICE CREAM

INGREDIENTS

500ml milk
250ml double cream
140g caster sugar
6 large egg yolks
½ teaspoon salt
1 tablespoon vanilla bean
    paste

This makes a very rich and creamy ice cream, perfect for an indulgent treat.

METHOD

1. Heat the milk and double cream in a non-stick pan until it is beginning to bubble.

2. Whisk the sugar into the egg yolks. Stir through the salt and vanilla to combine. Gradually pour the hot milk into the egg yolk mixture, stirring constantly.

3. Return the mix to the pan and cook over a low heat, constantly stirring until the mixture thickens to coat the back of a spoon or registers 75°C to 82°C.

4. Cover the surface of the custard with cling film or baking paper, then chill in the fridge until cold and ready to be churned.

EGGLESS BASE ICE CREAM

INGREDIENTS

600ml whole milk
60g skimmed milk powder
120g caster sugar
15g cornflour
1 tablespoon vanilla bean
    paste

This will create a slightly cleaner and fresher ice cream as it doesn't contain as much fat. Whatever flavours you add to this ice cream will come through stronger than with the custard base.

METHOD

1. Whisk 100ml of milk with the milk powder, sugar, cornflour and vanilla until combined. Gradually whisk through the remaining milk.

2. Pour this mixture into a pan over a high heat, constantly stirring until it bubbles and thickens. Cover the surface with cling film or baking paper and chill in the fridge until fridge cold and ready to be used.

SORBET

INGREDIENTS

100g caster sugar
100ml water
500g thin fruit purée (page 40)

This is a straightforward rule of thumb guide for making a sorbet from a fruit purée. This works well with mango, berries or stone fruits. Every type of fruit will have different sugar content, which will alter the taste and texture of the final product. Results may not always be entirely consistent when you change the fruit; however, it will always create delicious results.

METHOD

1. Make a simple syrup by stirring together the caster sugar and water over a high heat until it just begins to boil and the sugar has dissolved.

2. Remove from the heat and stir in the fruit purée. Cover and chill until fridge cold.

3. Churn the mixture as directed for ice creams (page 50).

ICE CREAM FLAVOURS
CHOCOLATE

INGREDIENTS

1 quantity ice cream base
100ml whole milk
20g cocoa powder
100g dark chocolate

METHOD

1. Make one of the ice cream bases outlined on page 51.

2. While the ice cream base is still warm, heat the milk and cocoa powder in a separate pan until it is beginning to bubble.

3. Remove from the heat and stir in the chocolate until melted and combined.

4. Whisk the warm chocolate mixture into the warm ice cream base before chilling and churning.

PISTACHIO

INGREDIENTS

1 quantity ice cream base
200g pistachios
   (or 150g pistachio paste
   + 50g pistachios)

METHOD

1. Add 150g of pistachios into a food processor and blitz until they are a very finely ground powder. The powder will begin to clump together; this is a good indication it is ready.

2. Add the ground pistachios or pistachio paste with the milk at the start of making your ice cream base, as outlined on page 51, then continue making and churning the base as normal.

3. Roughly chop the remaining 50g of pistachios and mix through the ice cream at the end of churning.

GINGERBREAD

INGREDIENTS

1 quantity ice cream base, but switch caster sugar for light brown sugar
1 teaspoon ground cinnamon
1 teaspoon ground ginger
200g sticky ginger cake, chilled (page 78)

METHOD

1. Make one of the ice cream bases outlined on page 51 using light brown sugar instead of caster sugar. Mix the ground cinnamon and ginger with the sugar when making the base.

2. Churn the ice cream, then crumble in and briefly mix through the ginger cake once the mixture has reached a soft-serve consistency.

COFFEE

INGREDIENTS

1 quantity ice cream base
3 tablespoons instant coffee
    powder

METHOD

1. Mix the coffee powder with
   3 tablespoons of milk into a paste.
   Add this into the remaining milk
   and make the ice cream base as
   outlined on page 51.

SALTED CARAMEL

INGREDIENTS

1 quantity ice cream base,
    but switch caster sugar for
    light brown sugar
1 quantity salted caramel
    sauce (low butter and
    high cream content),
    cooled (page 34)

METHOD

1. Make the ice cream base using
   light brown sugar instead of caster
   sugar, as outlined on page 51.

2. Drizzle the salted caramel sauce
   into the churning ice cream at
   the end of the churning. Don't
   overmix. You want some streaks
   of the sauce to remain in the ice
   cream.

CHAPTER 2
CAKES

When I think about baking for celebrations, I always think about baking cake. Birthdays, anniversaries, exam congratulations, leaving dos. All these call out for and welcome cake because it is so versatile and customisable to the unique event or person you are celebrating. I love this chapter's collection of recipes, and I trust the variety offered gives you great options to bake for most occasions and personal preferences.

ELDERFLOWER AND STRAWBERRY SWISS ROLL

INGREDIENTS

For the sponge

4 large eggs
110g caster sugar (plus
    additional for dusting)
1 teaspoon vanilla bean
    paste
110g self-raising flour (gf)

For the filling

200ml double cream
20g icing sugar
2 tablespoons elderflower
    cordial
1 lemon, zested
200g strawberries

For the decoration

Strawberries

Light sponge, zingy fresh cream and juicy strawberries combine to make this a delightful summery cake. You can also put this together from start to finish within an hour if you need to get a cake on the table – and fast. If you aim to achieve a tight spiral, you must slice the strawberries very thin and not overfill the sponge with cream. But if you are not so worried about the spiral, just fill it with as much cream as you want to eat!

METHOD

Preheat the oven to 170°C fan/ 180°C conventional/gas mark 4. Line a 33cm x 23cm Swiss roll tin with non-stick baking paper.

Make the sponge

1. In a stand mixer or using an electric hand mixer, whisk the eggs with the sugar and vanilla until they reach ribbon stage. It should be very thick and pale; you should be able to write a figure of 8 before the mixture sinks back in.

2. Sieve over the flour and gently fold in using a flexible spatula. Once there are no more pockets of flour, pour into the prepared tin and bake for 8 to 10 minutes or until lightly golden and quite actively bubbly.

3. While the cake is in the oven, cover a sheet of baking paper, slightly larger than the cake, with the additional caster sugar.

4. Once the sponge is baked, leave it to cool for 5 minutes in the tin. Turn out the warm sponge onto the sugar-covered baking paper. Use the baking paper to roll the sponge into a tight spiral, then unroll and leave to cool in between the baking paper sheets.

Make the filling

1. Whisk the cream to soft peaks with the icing sugar, cordial and lemon zest.

2. Slice the strawberries as thinly as you can. Place them on kitchen towel or a clean tea towel to absorb some excess moisture.

Assemble the Swiss roll

1. Spread an even layer of cream filling over the sponge reserving about one third for later. There is a trade-off between being generous with the filling and getting a tight spiral; you can decide which is more important. Lay the thinly sliced strawberries over the cream. Top with a further thin layer of cream, leaving some for later.

2. Start from one of the short sides and use the baking paper underneath to lift up the sponge, roll it onto itself and create a tight roll. Transfer to your serving plate with the join at the bottom. Use a sharp knife to slice off the ends to reveal the spiral.

3. Decorate with a line of strawberries along the cake, using the reserved cream to stick them down.

CRANACHAN CAKE

INGREDIENTS

For the cake
75g porridge oats (gf)
225g butter, softened
150g light brown sugar
150g clear honey
3 large eggs
225g self-raising flour (gf)
1 teaspoon baking powder
   (gf)
1 teaspoon salt

For the syrup soak
50g sugar
50ml water
50g clear honey
50ml whisky

For the filling
200ml double cream
3 tablespoons whisky
2 tablespoons clear honey
150g raspberries, fresh or
   frozen and defrosted

To assemble
1 quantity Italian meringue
   buttercream (page 27)
1 quantity oaty crumble (gf),
   (page 48)
300g raspberries

I had to put cranachan cake in this book. This is version 5.0 of my recipe, and it's my favourite version yet! Cranachan is a classic Scottish dessert typically made with oatmeal, raspberries, honey, a soft cheese called crowdie and whisky. We grew up with Mum making this for dessert on Burns night and St Andrew's Day. When we were young, she omitted the whisky, as you can do when you make this cake. The classic flavours of cranachan run through the whole cake, from the oat and honey sponge to the honey and whisky syrup soak.

Once I have all the components ready, stacking, filling and icing a layer cake like this is one of my favourite kitchen tasks. A turntable makes icing a tall cake a lot easier, but it isn't a necessity. Try to keep the layers as level as possible when stacking; a couple of skewed layers can lead to a very wonky leaning cake!

METHOD

Preheat the oven to 160°C fan/ 170°C conventional/gas mark 3.5. Grease and base line 4 x 18cm round sandwich tins or 2 x 18cm cake tins.

Make the cake
1. Blitz the oats in a food processor or blender until fine and powdery.

2. Cream together the softened butter and brown sugar until light. Add in the honey, eggs, flour, baking powder, salt and blitzed oats. Mix until fully combined.

3. Split the mixture evenly between the tins. Level them off and bake for about 20 minutes (4 tins) or 30 minutes (2 tins). A skewer should come out clean, and you should hear a gentle bubble. Allow to cool fully.

Make the syrup soak
1. Place the sugar, water, honey and whisky in a pan over a high heat. Stir until the mixture boils and the sugar has dissolved, then remove from the heat.

Make the filling
1. Whip the cream to soft peaks with the whisky and honey. Gently fold through the raspberries with their juice.

2. This is a good time to make your oaty crumble so it is ready for when you assemble the cake.

Continues overleaf . . .

Assemble the cake

1. Slice the top crust off the sponges. If you only have 2 cakes, slice them in half to create 4 layers. Brush the open tops of the sponges with syrup; be generous and use all the syrup.
2. Place a layer of sponge down on your serving plate. Pipe Italian meringue buttercream to create a ring around the inside perimeter of the sponge; fill this with the cream filling and sprinkle over some oaty crumble, saving some to decorate your cake too.
3. Repeat this layering process two more times. Place the final layer onto the cakes with the flat, unsoaked side facing up.
4. Dirty ice the entire cake by spreading a very thin layer of buttercream all around it. Place it in the fridge for at least 30 minutes to firm up.
5. Cover the cake again in more buttercream to neaten up the finish. I like to create a ridged effect by running the end of a palette knife all the way up and around the cake while spinning it on a turntable.
6. Take your leftover oaty crumble and press some into the lower portion of the cake. Sprinkle the rest around the top edge of the cake.
7. Finish the cake by standing raspberries over the top.

CHOCOLATE AND FIG FRASIER CAKE

INGREDIENTS

For the chocolate Genoise

3 large eggs
100g caster sugar
70g self-raising flour (gf)
30g cocoa powder
35g butter, melted and cooled

For the honey syrup

50g honey
25ml water

For the vanilla crème mousseline

200ml whole milk
2 large egg yolks
50g caster sugar
20g cornflour
1 tablespoon vanilla bean paste
50g butter, softened

For the chocolate ganache crème pat

200ml whole milk
2 large egg yolks
50g caster sugar
15g cornflour
10g cocoa powder
2 teaspoons vanilla bean paste
50ml double cream
50g dark chocolate

To assemble

8 figs
10g cocoa powder

Frasier is a classic French cake that is instantly recognisable from the stunning design of strawberries standing at attention around its perimeter. I have taken this design approach and applied it to another stunning fruit; figs. I love bakes decorated like this. It highlights the detail and beauty of the produce used.

It's not just about the look, though; the eating is also very enjoyable. Simple flavours are running through the bake, fig, vanilla, chocolate and a little honey. The creamy fillings are rich and indulgent, so the cake lends itself more towards a sit-down dessert rather than a slice to have with a cup of tea in the afternoon.

METHOD

Preheat the oven to 160°C fan/ 170°C conventional/gas mark 3. Grease and base line a deep 20cm cake tin. Line the sides of another 20cm cake ring or tin (preferably loose-bottomed) with a strip of acetate. This is not necessary but does turn the cake out more cleanly.

Make the chocolate Genoise

1. Whisk the eggs and sugar on full speed with an electric hand whisk or stand mixer until it's very thick and pale and holds a strong trail. This will take about 5 minutes.

2. Sieve over the flour and cocoa powder and gently fold in using a flexible spatula. Once almost fully incorporated, pour in the cooled melted butter around the side of the bowl and fold in until just combined.

3. Pour the mixture into the greased tin and bake for about 25 minutes or until a skewer comes out clean and you can hear a gentle foamy bubble. Cool in the tin for about 5 minutes, then turn out to cool fully.

4. Once cool, slice the cake in half horizontally to create two even layers.

Make the honey syrup

1. Stir the honey and water together in a pan over a high heat until it just begins to boil.

Make the vanilla crème mousseline

1. Make a vanilla crème pat as instructed on page 46, and using all the ingredients detailed here apart from the softened butter. Cover and leave to cool to room temperature.

2. Whisk the cooled crème pat to smooth it out.

3. Whisk the softened butter for a few minutes until considerably lightened in colour and texture.

4. Whisk the butter into the crème pat, adding it gradually until fully combined.

Make the chocolate ganache

1. Make a chocolate crème pat as instructed on page 46, using all the ingredients listed here, excluding the double cream and chocolate. Leave to cool to room temperature.

Continues overleaf . . .

2. Heat the cream in a separate pan until just boiling. Add in the chocolate off the heat and stir to make your ganache. Cool the ganache until it reaches room temperature and is thick, but still spreadable.

3. Whisk the room temperature ganache through the crème pat until smooth.

Assemble the cake

1. Place the top layer of cake into the acetate-lined cake ring. Brush the cut side of the sponge with honey syrup.

2. Cut the figs in half lengthways. Place them onto the edge of the sponge in the cake ring, pressing the figs' flat side against the side of the tin. Press them in tightly together, you may need to slice a fig half into a smaller portion to fill in the tin. If you have any left over, chop them into a small dice.

3. Fill a piping bag with the crème mousseline. Pipe it over the bottom of the cake and in between the figs. Use a palette knife to spread out the crème making sure it fills any gaps in the figs. Top the centre of the crème with the chopped figs.

4. Cover the figs and crème mousseline with the chocolate ganache crème pat and level off. The chocolate should not be visible from the sides of the cake when turned out.

5. Brush the open side of the last layer of sponge with honey syrup. Place into the ring with the flat side facing up. Sieve a dusting of cocoa powder over the cake and chill in the fridge for at least an hour.

6. Slide the ring off the cake and peel off the acetate, or run a palette knife around the tin and lift the ring off, if not using acetate. Decorate the cake with more figs.

VICTORIA SANDWICH

INGREDIENTS

For the cake

150g butter, softened
150g caster sugar
150g self-raising flour (gf)
3 large eggs
1½ teaspoons baking
    powder (gf)
1½ teaspoons vanilla bean
    paste (or other flavour,
    e.g. lemon extract)

For the filling

150ml double cream
15g icing sugar
150g jam or curd
    of your choice
    (e.g. lemon curd)

I think the Victoria sandwich is the ultimate British bake. It's the all-time go-to cake to enjoy with an afternoon cup of tea. This cake carries a lot of memories for me, as I imagine it does for many others. It was the first cake I ever made with my mum and the first bake I could make without using a written recipe. My mum taught me the phrase '4, 4, 4 and 2', referring to the quantities of butter, sugar and self-raising flour in ounces and the number of eggs needed. Remember that, and you can make a Victoria sandwich without even needing to crack out a cookbook.

We should probably update to the metric system, so here you go: '100, 100, 100 and 2.' I've added in '1 and 1' at the end for the teaspoon each of baking powder and vanilla. Remember those ratios, and after a few practices of the technique, you can get a Victoria sponge on the table in under 10 minutes of hands-on time and no cookbook in sight.

I have increased the ingredient volumes by 50% for this recipe to give a slightly deeper cake, which shows you how simple it is to scale this recipe.

The cake shown here is a lemon Victoria sandwich. I switched the vanilla bean paste in the batter for lemon extract and filled it with lemon curd and cream.

METHOD

Preheat the oven to 160°C fan/ 170°C conventional/gas mark 3.5. Grease and base line 2 x 18cm cake tins.

Make the cake

1. Cream together the butter and sugar until considerably lighter and fluffier. This will take you about 5 minutes.

2. Add in all the remaining ingredients and mix until just fully combined.

3. Split the mixture evenly between the 2 tins, smoothing out the top with a spoon or palette knife. Bake for 15 to 20 minutes or until a skewer comes out clean and you can hear the cake very gently bubbling. Allow the cakes to cool slightly in the tin and then turn out onto a wire rack.

Make the filling and assemble

1. Whisk the cream to soft peaks with the icing sugar.

2. Spread the jam or curd in an even layer over one of the sponges. Top this with the cream and encourage it to spread to the cake's edge, leaving some of the curd or jam visible.

3. Top with the second sponge and dust with icing sugar if desired.

GRAPEFRUIT GIN DRIZZLE CAKE

INGREDIENTS

For the cake

175g unsalted butter,
    softened
200g caster sugar
100g self-raising flour (gf)
100g ground almonds
½ teaspoon baking powder
    (gf)
4 large eggs
1 grapefruit, zested and
    juiced (1 tablespoon)

For the syrup

100g caster sugar
70ml grapefruit juice (from
    your zested grapefruit)
2 tablespoons gin

For the icing

150g icing sugar
2 tablespoons reserved
    syrup

To decorate

1 grapefruit, sliced

Drenched in sweet botanical syrup with a bitter edge, this cake is right on the line of how moist a cake can be. It will stay soft for at least 5 days if well covered, so it's a useful bake if you like to prep ahead. Using a drizzle is also a good safety measure when baking a cake. There is virtually no way you can create a dry sponge once you have drowned it in a delicious syrup. The gin and grapefruit take this away from being overwhelmingly sweet, and I think the distinctive flavour is quite exciting. It's something you don't generally come across in cake form!

METHOD

Preheat the oven to 160°C fan/ 170°C conventional/gas mark 3.5. Grease and line a 900g loaf tin, with a long sheet of baking paper leaving overhang on the long sides of the tin.

Make the cake

1. Cream the butter and sugar until light. Add in the remaining cake ingredients and mix until combined. Add to the loaf tin and spread out evenly.

2. Bake for about 45 minutes or until a skewer comes out clean.

Make the syrup

1. While the cake is in the oven, make the syrup. Stir the sugar, grapefruit juice and gin in a saucepan over a high heat until the sugar has dissolved and the mixture boils. Remove from the heat. Set aside 2 tablespoons of the syrup.

2. Once the cake has baked, leave it to cool for 10 minutes in the tin. Poke it all over with your testing skewer and pour over the main, larger portion of syrup. Leave it to soak in as it cools completely in the tin. The cake sometimes sinks a bit in the tin. Don't worry if it sinks on you, it still tastes delicious!

Make the icing

1. Mixing together the icing sugar with the reserved syrup to make a thick but fluid consistency. You may not need all the syrup, so add it gradually.

2. Remove the cooled cake from the tin and cover with the icing, encouraging a few drips around the edges. Top with some grapefruit slices.

LEMON, CLEMENTINE AND ALMOND CAKE

INGREDIENTS

For the topping
1 clementine
1 lemon
150ml water
100g sugar

For the cake
2 clementines
1 lemon
4 large eggs
180g caster sugar
100ml olive oil
150g ground almonds
90g self-raising flour (gf)
1½ teaspoons baking
    powder (gf)

Using whole clementines and lemons in the cake batter brightens the flavour. There is a slight bitterness to the resulting taste, which I like, but you can omit the lemon in the batter and replace it with another clementine if you're not a fan. The resulting cake is soft and moist, and it keeps very well because of the ground almonds and oil. Covered and left at room temperature, it will stay moist for a good 5 days.

METHOD

Preheat the oven to 160°C fan/ 170°C conventional/gas mark 3.5. Grease and base line a 20cm cake tin.

Make the topping

1. Slice a clementine and a lemon into fairly thin rounds. Stir the water and sugar together in a pan over a high heat. Once dissolved add in the lemon and clementine slices. Simmer for about 15 minutes, until they are soft and look slightly translucent. Drain and set aside; making sure to reserve the syrup for later.

2. Arrange the slices in a single layer on the bottom of your prepared cake tin.

Make the cake

1. Place the whole clementines and lemon in a saucepan with a lid. Cover with water and simmer for 15 to 25 minutes until very soft. Drain the fruits, slice them in half and discard any pips. Leave to cool.

2. Whisk together the eggs and sugar in a stand mixer until light and foamy, not taking the mix all the way to ribbon stage. Stream in the oil while still whisking.

3. Blitz the cooled fruit in a food processor to a chunky purée. Add 200g of the purée with the almonds, flour and baking powder to the egg mixture and fold through. You don't have to be overly gentle here.

4. Pour into the tin on top of your citrus slices. Bake for about 40 to 45 minutes, until it passes the skewer test and has a gentle bubble when you listen to it.

5. Allow to cool in the tin for 10 to 15 minutes, then remove. The bottom of the cake, with its pattern of sliced citrus, now becomes the top.

6. Brush a little reserved syrup over the top of the cake to give it a shiny finish before serving.

RASPBERRY, PISTACHIO AND CHOCOLATE MARBLE CAKE

INGREDIENTS

220g butter, softened
220g caster sugar

For the raspberry cake
140g creamed mix
70g self-raising flour (gf)
1 large egg
40g raspberry jam
½ teaspoon baking powder
   (gf)
10g freeze-dried raspberry
   powder
2 tablespoons milk

For the pistachio cake
160g creamed mix
50g pistachios
1 large egg
35g ground almonds
35g self-raising flour (gf)
½ teaspoon baking powder
   (gf)
2 tablespoons milk
Green gel food colouring,
   tiny amount

For the chocolate cake
140g creamed mix
20g cocoa powder
1 large egg
20g self-raising flour (gf)
30g ground almonds
2 tablespoons milk
½ teaspoon baking powder
   (gf)

For the topping
150g icing sugar
20g pistachios, chopped
5g freeze-dried raspberry
   pieces

I've had to refrain from using this all-star flavour trio too much in this book! The combo of raspberry, pistachio and chocolate works beautifully in basically every baking setting, so I could have happily written an entire chapter featuring these as the only flavours.

This cake showcases the combination very well. Each of the cake mixes results in a slightly different texture, and thanks to the marbling, every bite combines 3 different flavours with those 3 different textures making it an intriguing eat. The overall texture of the cake is also very satisfying. There are lots of ground nuts running through the chocolate and pistachio cakes which cling onto moisture and give body while remaining tender.

METHOD

Preheat the oven to 160°C fan/ 170°C conventional/gas mark 3.5. Grease a 20cm Bundt tin well with a little melted and cooled butter.

1. Cream the butter and sugar until light and creamy. Weigh the creamed butter and sugar mix between 3 bowls as outlined in the ingredient list for each cake.

2. Make the raspberry cake batter by mixing through all of the remaining ingredients until well combined.

3. Make the pistachio cake batter. Blitz the pistachios in a food processor until they resemble the texture of ground almonds. Mix all the ingredients through the creamed butter and sugar.

4. Make the chocolate cake batter by sieving the cocoa powder over the creamed butter and sugar and mixing through with all the remaining ingredients.

5. Spoon alternating small portions of the 3 mixtures into the Bundt tin until you have used all of the batters. Use a table knife to briefly swirl the mixtures together, creating that distinctive marbled look.

6. Bake for about 35 minutes or until a skewer comes out clean. Leave to cool for 10 to 15 minutes before removing from the tin, then cool fully on a wire rack.

Make the topping
1. Stir together the icing sugar and 2 tablespoons of water to create a thick but fluid icing. Drizzle this over the ridges of the cooled cake. Decorate with chopped pistachios and freeze-dried raspberry pieces.

DARK STOUT LOAF CAKE

INGREDIENTS

For the cake

175g self-raising flour (gf)
50g cocoa powder
1 teaspoon bicarbonate of
    soda
1 teaspoon salt
150g butter
150g dark muscovado sugar
40g treacle
2 large eggs, beaten
150ml stout (substitute for
    cola if gf)

For the frosting

75g butter
150g icing sugar
150g cream cheese

I first enjoyed a stout cake like this in a café in Edinburgh, Thomas J Walls, and knew I needed to recreate it. Stout has chocolate, coffee and treacle notes that carry right through this bake and make the flavour reminiscent of, but different to, a simple chocolate cake. A straightforward but reasonably complete description of the sponge is 'dark and rich', so the pairing with cream cheese frosting is perfect as it brings a tang to cut against the cake.

Gluten-free stout can be tricky to source, so cola is a brilliant substitute to make this gluten-free or teetotal. Some colas contain barley and are not gluten-free. If making this cake gluten-free, make sure you buy a cola without barley.

METHOD

Preheat the oven to 160°C fan/ 170°C conventional/gas mark 3. Grease and line a 900g loaf tin with a long sheet of baking paper leaving overhang on the long sides of the tin.

Make the cake

1. Sieve the flour, cocoa powder and bicarbonate of soda into a large mixing bowl, then add the salt.

2. Gently heat the butter, sugar and treacle in a pan until melted. Pour this into the dry ingredients and stir together.

3. Whisk through the eggs, followed by the stout (or cola), adding it gradually. Pour into the prepared loaf tin.

4. Bake for about 40 minutes or until a skewer comes out clean but sings with a consistent moist bubble.

Make the frosting

1. Beat the butter until smooth and light. Sieve over the icing sugar in 3 batches, beating for 2 minutes after each addition.

2. Add the cream cheese a third at a time and mix each batch through gently until just combined.

3. Spread the frosting over the cooled loaf cake.

CHOCOLATE BIRTHDAY CAKE

INGREDIENTS

For the cake

220g plain flour (gf)

100g cocoa powder

1½ teaspoons
baking powder (gf)

1½ teaspoons bicarbonate
of soda

350g caster sugar

1 teaspoon salt

2 teaspoons instant coffee
powder

2 teaspoons vanilla extract

2 large eggs

240ml milk

140ml oil

180ml boiling water

For the ganache

300g double cream

200g dark chocolate

For the Chantilly

100g double cream

15g icing sugar

1 teaspoon vanilla bean
paste

This is my favourite chocolate cake recipe. It is stupendously moist with a rich, sweet chocolate taste. This whole bake is very simple to make, doesn't involve much washing-up and is a crowd-pleaser near certain to go down a storm at any birthday bash.

METHOD

Preheat the oven to 170°C fan/ 180°C conventional/gas mark 4. Grease and base line 2 x 20cm round cake tins.

Make the cake

1. Sieve the flour, cocoa powder, baking powder and bicarbonate of soda into a bowl. Add in the sugar, salt and coffee powder. Whisk in the vanilla, eggs, milk and oil until smooth.

2. Measure out the boiling water and slowly stream it into the mixture, whisking constantly.

3. Pour the thin batter into the prepared tins. Bake for about 40 minutes or until a skewer comes out with only a few moist crumbs.

Make the ganache

1. Make the chocolate ganache as instructed on page 30. Leave to cool to room temperature so it is thick and spreadable, then fill a piping bag with it.

Make the Chantilly

1. Whisk the cream with the icing sugar and vanilla to soft peaks.

Assemble the cake

1. Trim down the dome of the cakes. Stick one cake down on your serving plate with a dod of ganache.

2. Pipe a rim of ganache around the perimeter of the bottom cake. Then fill the space you have created with the Chantilly.

3. Place the other cake on top with the flat bottom edge facing up. Chill in the fridge to firm up.

4. Pipe the rest of the ganache around the cake and use a palette knife to spread it out. I like to use the knife to swoosh and swoop the ganache around the cake. If the ganache is a little too firm to spread, gently warm the knife in hot water to make it easier to spread.

STICKY ICED GINGER CAKE

INGREDIENTS

225g self-raising flour (gf)
1 tablespoon ground ginger
2 teaspoons ground
  cinnamon
1 teaspoon bicarbonate of
  soda
1 teaspoon salt
150g butter
150g golden syrup
150g dark muscovado sugar
2 large eggs, beaten
150ml ginger beer

For the icing
150g icing sugar
2 tablespoons ginger beer

For decoration
20g crystallised stem ginger

I feel this is not always a particularly popular cake, but a good sticky iced ginger cake is one of my favourites. My nostalgic association with ginger cake is quite bizarrely connected to a badminton centre in Glasgow. After being knocked out from a badminton competition, I would get a slice of this home-baked cake as a treat for the journey back to Edinburgh. It's the most unlikely place, but I still consider that 50p square of ginger cake the best you can get! I've tried to get as close as possible to those standards with this recipe.

METHOD

Preheat the oven to 170°C fan/ 180°C conventional/gas mark 4. Grease and base line a 20cm square cake tin.

1. Sieve the flour, ground ginger, ground cinnamon and bicarbonate of soda into a large mixing bowl with the salt.

2. Heat the butter, golden syrup and sugar until just melted. Pour this into the dry mix and stir until smooth. Whisk in the eggs, then whisk in the ginger beer to make a very thin batter.

3. Pour into the cake tin and bake for 30 to 35 minutes. Very few moist crumbs can remain on the skewer when testing, and it should sound more bubbly than a typical cake but not wet.

Ice and decorate your cake
1. Mix together the ginger beer and icing sugar to a fluid consistency. Pour over the cooled cake and leave to set before slicing into squares, and decorating with crystallised stem ginger, if desired.

UPSIDE DOWN BANANA CAKE

INGREDIENTS

For the topping
2 large bananas
100g caster sugar
50g butter
25g walnuts, chopped

For the cake
2 large bananas (about 200g)
100g soft brown sugar
2 large eggs
100ml oil
150g self-raising flour (gf)
1 teaspoon baking powder (gf)
½ teaspoon salt
75g walnuts, chopped

I have tried to give a regular banana bread a bit of an upgrade by combining it with a tarte Tatin-inspired topping. The caramelised bananas on top are sticky and shiny, and lift this from regular banana bread to a more deluxe version.

Everyone will be fighting over the corner pieces to make sure they nab the lion's share of the deeply browned, caramelised bananas that sit on the cake edges. So, if you're the baker, make sure you save yourself a corner before passing it around your friends!

METHOD

Preheat the oven to 170°C fan/ 180°C conventional/gas mark 4. Grease and base line a 20cm square tin.

Make the topping
1. Slice the bananas into coins that are about 1.5cm thick.

2. Make a dry caramel with the sugar (page 34). Once deep amber, stir through the butter. Pour this caramel into the base of the tin.

3. Arrange the banana slices over the caramel in the base of the cake tin. Fill in any gaps with chopped walnuts.

Make the cake
1. Roughly mash the bananas. Add to a bowl with the sugar, eggs and oil; whisk to combine.

2. Stir through the flour, baking powder, salt and chopped walnuts until no lumps of flour are visible.

3. Pour this mix into the prepared tin over the bananas. Bake for about 30 minutes.

4. Cool in the tin for about 10 minutes before turning out while still warm. Serve with the caramelised bananas showing off on top.

CHESTNUT AND PEAR CAKE

INGREDIENTS

For the Genoise sponge
5 large eggs
175g caster sugar
175g self-raising flour (gf)
½ teaspoon ground
    cinnamon
60g butter, melted and
    cooled

For the poached pears
300ml water
175g caster sugar
1 teaspoon ground
    cinnamon
1 teaspoon vanilla bean
    paste
1 lemon, peeled and halved
2 large pears

For the chestnut cream
250g sweetened chestnut
    purée (tins available
    online)
300ml double cream
1 teaspoon vanilla bean
    paste

For the covering
1 quantity Italian or Swiss
    meringue (see page 27)

For this cake, I took inspiration from the classic French dessert, Mont Blanc, a dessert of sweet chestnut purée with whipped cream served on a meringue or biscuit. This cake's soft interior is covered in snowy white meringue to evoke the image of the bake's mountainous namesake. Sweetened chestnut purée has a unique creamy, nutty autumnal flavour and pairs very well with gently cinnamony poached pears. If you've never tried sweet chestnut, give this cake a go for an autumn or winter treat; the flavour is intriguing and delicious.

METHOD

Preheat the oven to 160°C fan/ 170°C conventional/gas mark 3.5. Grease and base line 2 x 18cm deep cake tins.

Make the Genoise sponge
1. Whisk the eggs and sugar on full speed with an electric hand whisk or stand mixer until the mix is very thick and pale and holds a strong ribbon trail.

2. Sieve over the flour and cinnamon and gently fold in using a flexible spatula. Once the flour is almost fully incorporated, pour the butter around the side of the bowl and fold in until just combined.

3. Pour the mixture into the tins and bake for about 25 minutes or until a skewer comes out clean and you can hear a gentle foamy bubble. Cool in the tins for about 5 minutes, then turn out to cool fully.

Poach the pears
1. Bring the water, sugar, cinnamon, vanilla, lemon peel and halves to a gentle simmer in a large pan.

2. Peel, core and slice the pears into about ½ cm slices. Place these in the simmering liquid, cover and cook for 10 to 15 minutes. Once they are soft yet still holding their shape, drain the pears.

3. Return the syrup to the pan and boil for 2 minutes. Leave to cool.

Make the chestnut cream
1. Pass the chestnut purée through a sieve and whisk to smooth it out.

2. Add the cream and vanilla to the purée and whisk to medium-firm peaks.

Assemble the cake
1. Trim the top off each sponge to flatten and then slice into 2 so you now have 4 layers.

2. Brush some cooled syrup from the pears over each layer of cake.

3. Place one layer of cake down on a serving board. Cover with a layer of chestnut cream and top this with a layer of poached pears followed by a further thin layer of chestnut cream. Repeat until you reach the top layer. Make sure the final layer of cake is a bottom half and place this on upside down, so there is a sharp, finished edge to the cake top.

4. Spread a very thin layer of the chestnut cream around the cake with a palette knife. Chill in the fridge for about 20 minutes.

5. Take the cake out the fridge and cover with a layer of meringue. Use a blowtorch sporadically around the cake to brown the meringue in parts; this isn't essential, though!

CHAPTER 3
PASTRY

Pastry is all about texture and simple flavour on which you can layer exciting fillings to create delicious bakes. The chapter starts with fresh, fruity bakes and progresses through to richer and more comforting recipes, showing how broadly and imaginatively you can apply such a simple base recipe.

LEMON TART

INGREDIENTS

1 quantity sweet shortcrust
    pastry (page 18) (gf)
4 to 5 large lemons, zested
    and juiced (approx.
    200g juice)
150g caster sugar
170g double cream
4 large eggs, beaten
2 large egg yolks

I struggle to look past a lemon tart on a dessert menu. It's the ultimate showcase of restraint and simplicity in baking, and I think that's what makes it one of the most beautiful bakes possible. There is nowhere to hide in baking a tart like this; the ultimate goal is a gentle soft set texture and smooth top.

However, things don't always work out . . . issues can happen and that's fine. If the top cracks, it was likely over baked; if it looks bubbly, you didn't remove enough bubbles before baking; if the base is soggy, the pastry case was likely not blind baked for long enough. If any of these issues arise, the result will still be a puckeringly tart and moreishly sweet and creamy dessert that will be a joy to eat. Next time, you can adjust your baking to rectify these small mistakes.

METHOD

Preheat the oven to 180°C fan/
190°C conventional/gas mark 5.

1. Blind bake a 20–23cm pastry case
   as instructed on page 18, making
   sure to give the pastry case an egg
   wash for the uncovered bake.

Reduce the oven temperature to
150°C fan/160°C conventional/gas
mark 3.

1. Sieve the lemon juice into a bowl
   and weigh it; it should lie between
   180–220g. Whisk the sugar into
   the lemon juice until dissolved.
   Lightly whisk through the zest,
   double cream and beaten eggs
   and yolks until fully combined.
   Pour this mixture into a jug, let it
   settle for a couple of minutes, then
   skim off the bubbles from the top.

2. Pour the filling into the pastry case
   over the back of a spoon. Make
   sure to pour the final bits of filling
   into the case with the tart half in
   the oven, to avoid spillages as
   you move the tart to the oven.
   Bake for 25 to 30 minutes or until
   the mixture gently wobbles in the
   centre when shaken lightly.

3. Allow the tart to cool in the tin
   for 5 minutes, then remove from
   the tin and slide off the base
   onto a wire rack to cool. This will
   help prevent soggy pastry. Once
   cooled to room temperature, chill
   in the fridge before serving.

MANGO, COCONUT AND WHITE CHOCOLATE TART

INGREDIENTS

1 quantity sweet shortcrust
pastry (page 18) (gf)

For the coconut filling
25g butter, softened
25g caster sugar
30g coconut cream (use the
solid top from a tin of
coconut milk or replace
with more butter)
30g self-raising flour (gf)
1 large egg white
45g desiccated coconut
½ teaspoon vanilla extract
¼ teaspoon salt
40g white chocolate chips

For the mango curd
350g mango purée
(page 40), or tinned
mango pulp
3 large egg yolks
75g sugar
100g butter, cubed

For decoration
1 mango
50g toasted coconut flakes

For me, this tart feels exotic with its bold mango and coconut flavours. The tart combines a silky mango curd over a texturally interesting coconut sponge base. Before making the curd, it's worth reducing a portion of the mango purée. This considerably intensifies the flavour and brightens the tart. I think mango is a flavour that needs to be punchy: a weak mango flavour is pretty dull, but intense mango is fun and exciting!

Instead of making mango purée myself, I use tinned mango pulp. It's not overly expensive, tastes brilliant and eliminates a tedious step in the baking process.

METHOD

Preheat the oven to 180°C fan/
190°C conventional/gas mark 5.

1. Blind bake a 20cm pastry case as instructed on page 18.

Make the coconut filling
1. Cream together the butter and sugar until light and fluffy (this will take between 3 and 5 minutes).

2. Add in the coconut cream, flour, egg white, coconut, vanilla and salt and mix through until combined.

3. Spread this over the pastry case and press the white chocolate chips into the mixture. Bake for about 15 minutes or until a skewer comes out clean.

4. Remove the tart from the tin and leave it to cool on a wire rack.

Make the mango curd
1. Place 275g of the mango purée in a pan on a high heat and boil to reduce it by about half, stirring frequently to prevent it burning. Take off the heat and weigh it out. Add the remaining non-reduced purée, so the total weight is 190g.

2. Whisk together the egg yolks and sugar. Then whisk through the mango purée and pour this into a pan over a low heat. Stir constantly until it is thick and reaches 75–82°C.

3. Take the curd off the heat. Whisk in the butter, a few cubes at a time, until the curd is smooth and shiny.

4. Pour the curd into the tart case and level off. Place in the fridge to set for at least 2 hours.

Decorate the tart
1. Chop the fresh mango into chunks and slices.

2. Decorate the top of the tart with the mango and toasted coconut flakes sweeping around one side.

APPLE GALETTE

1 quantity sweet shortcrust
    pastry (page 18) (gf)

For the frangipane
50g butter, softened
50g light brown sugar
1 large egg
½ teaspoon ground
    cinnamon
½ teaspoon salt
75g ground almonds
25g self-raising flour (gf)

For the apple filling
4 medium eating apples
50g light brown sugar
30g butter

To assemble
1 egg, beaten
30g demerara sugar
2 tablespoons apricot jam

A galette is a free-form tart made without a tin. This shaping gives the tart a rustic feel and is easier to achieve if you haven't quite mastered your tart lining skills yet. Each galette will be unique depending on how thinly you slice the apples, how large you roll out the pastry, how many folds are in the pastry creating the crust, or if there are any gaps allowing some of the apple caramel to be released. This is not a bake to be precious about; asymmetry and informality are what make this beautiful.

The simple taste of the galette, however, is even better than the design. Gentle cinnamon and almonds with sweet apples and buttery pastry. Buy in-season apples with a good bite, and the taste will not disappoint. I genuinely can't think of a pudding I would rather serve to friends and family directly from the centre of the table along with a scoop of vanilla ice cream (see page 50).

METHOD

Preheat the oven to 180°C fan/ 190°C conventional/gas mark 5. Line a baking tray with non-stick baking paper.

Make the frangipane
1. Cream the butter and sugar until fluffy. Add in all the remaining ingredients and stir to combine.

2. Roll the pastry out on a lightly floured surface to about ½ cm thick. Then cut a rough circle from the dough about 30cm in diameter. Place this on your baking tray.

3. Spread the frangipane over the pastry leaving a 5cm border all the way around the edge.

Make the apple filling
1. Core and quarter the apples, but keep the peel on. Slice each quarter into thin slices and fan these out from each quarter over the frangipane. Repeat for all the apples making sure to cover all the frangipane. Sprinkle the sugar over the apples and dot over with small pieces of butter.

Assemble the galette
1. Lift up the edge of the pastry and cover the edges of the apples all the way around the tart. The pastry will fold over itself; this adds to the informal look. Brush the pastry with egg wash and sprinkle with demerara sugar.

2. Bake for 30 to 35 minutes or until the pastry is golden and the apples are soft. Slide the galette and baking paper onto a cooling rack straight from the oven.

3. Gently warm the apricot jam and brush a light covering over the apples with a pastry brush to give them a shine. Serve and eat hot from the oven or cold later.

NECTARINE AND THYME TARTE TATIN

INGREDIENTS

1 quantity rough puff pastry
  (page 14) (gf)

For the filling
175g sugar
2 tablespoons water
70g butter
1 teaspoon flaky salt
1 tablespoon fresh thyme
  leaves, plus extra to
  decorate
6 large nectarines
40g toasted flaked almonds,
  plus extra to decorate

Putting thyme in a dessert might sound a little weird, but trust me – it does work! The subtle fragrance of the thyme sits very well with the creamy sweet nectarine. This recipe also works nicely with any other stone fruits.

Tarte Tatin is a bake that needs to be served hot, straight from the oven. At that moment, the fruit will be shiny, covered in a buttery caramel coating, and the pastry will be crisp as it won't have time to soften under the juicy fruits once turned out. The best part of a Tatin has got to be the edge of the pastry. This is a little thicker and gets covered in a sticky caramel in which it sits when baking. Fortunately, everyone gets an equal share of this golden edge when sharing a round Tatin.

METHOD

Preheat the oven to 190°C fan/ 200°C conventional/gas mark 6.

1. Stir together the sugar and water in an oven-safe frying pan (approx. 23cm) over a high heat. Stir until all the sugar has dissolved, then leave to bubble and deepen to a dark amber. Occasionally swirl the pan if the caramel is colouring unevenly.

2. Once the sugar is deep amber, add the butter, salt and thyme off the heat and stir until melted and combined.

3. If you do not have an oven-safe frying pan, make the caramel in a regular pan and pour into a 23cm round cake tin.

4. Slice the nectarines in half around the stone, discard the stone. Lay them on top of the caramel, some skin side down, some cut side down around the perimeter of the tin, all tightly packed together.

5. Once you have covered the edge of the tin, cut the remaining nectarine halves in half again and fill in the centre tightly. Sprinkle over the almonds to fill in any gaps. Mound up the filling with any remaining fruit.

6. Roll out the rough puff pastry on a lightly floured surface to about ½ cm thick. Cut a rough circle from this with a diameter about 2cm wider than your tin. Roll this up over your rolling pin, then unroll over the nectarines and caramel. Use a table knife to tuck the edges of the pastry down the sides of the nectarines to the bottom of the tin or pan. Cut a cross into the centre of the pastry and bake for 40 to 45 minutes until the pastry is a deep brown.

7. Once baked, remove the tart from the oven. Hold the pastry down and pour out any excess juice from the side of the tin into a saucepan. Boil this syrup for 2 minutes, so it thickens slightly.

8. While still hot, place a serving plate over the top of the tin or pan and invert the tarte Tatin. Brush the top with the reduced syrup and sprinkle over some additional thyme leaves and flaked almonds.

RHUBARB AND GINGER BAKEWELL TART

INGREDIENTS

For the pastry
1 quantity sweet shortcrust
  pastry (page 18) (gf)
1 teaspoon ground ginger

For the roasted rhubarb
100g rhubarb
20g sugar

For the stewed rhubarb
150g rhubarb, chopped
3 tablespoons rhubarb and
  ginger cordial (substitute
  orange juice here if you
  prefer)
35g caster sugar
10g cornflour mixed with
  2 teaspoons water

For the frangipane
100g butter, softened
100g caster sugar
75g self-raising flour (gf)
2 large eggs
125g ground almonds
1 teaspoon ground ginger
2 tablespoons rhubarb and
  ginger cordial (optional)
25g flaked almonds,
  to scatter over the
  frangipane

For the icing
50g icing sugar
2 to 3 teaspoons rhubarb
  and ginger cordial (or
  orange juice)

I am a big fan of anything with frangipane, so Bakewell tart is one of my favourites. This Bakewell is a little unique in that I've switched out the raspberry jam for stewed rhubarb. Vibrant pink forced rhubarb is perfect in this bake. Forced rhubarb is slightly sweeter and softer than its hardier late-season cousin and carries the beautiful colour that adds to the aesthetic of this bake. If you can't get hold of pink forced rhubarb, I would recommend adding an extra 20g of sugar to the stewed rhubarb – and your tart will still taste great.

METHOD

Preheat the oven to 180°C fan/190°C conventional/gas mark 5.

Make the pastry
1. Make and blind bake a 20–23cm pastry case as instructed on page 18. Add the ground ginger into the dough along with the flour.

Roast the rhubarb
1. Cut the rhubarb into roughly 4cm lengths. Place in a rimmed baking tray and sprinkle over the sugar.

2. Roast in the oven for about 10 minutes so it's beginning to soften while still holding its shape.

3. Lift the rhubarb onto a sheet of paper towel to cool.

Reduce the oven to 160°C fan/170°C conventional/gas mark 3.5.

Stew the rhubarb
1. Stir together the chopped rhubarb, cordial and sugar in a pan over a medium heat.

2. Simmer for about 5 minutes or until the rhubarb is beginning to break down. Add the cornflour and water mixture and stir in. Cook until the mixture looks jammy. Set aside to cool.

Make the frangipane
1. Cream together the butter and sugar until light and fluffy.

2. Add in the flour, eggs, ground almonds, ginger and cordial and mix until combined.

Assemble and bake
1. Spread the cooled stewed rhubarb over the base of the pastry case. Top this with the frangipane and level off. I find it easiest to pipe over the frangipane from the outside in. Press the roasted rhubarb into the frangipane and scatter over the flaked almonds. Bake for about 35 minutes until the frangipane feels set in the centre when gently pressed with your finger. Remove from the tin to cool on a wire rack.

2. Make the icing by mixing the icing sugar with the cordial until you achieve a thick fluid consistency. Drizzle the icing over the top of the cooled tart with bold strokes.

LIME AND CHOCOLATE MERINGUE PIES

INGREDIENTS

1 quantity chocolate sweet
   shortcrust pastry
   (page 18) (gf)

For the filling
4 large egg yolks
50g caster sugar
1 tin condensed milk (397g)
150ml double cream
4 to 6 limes, zested and
   juiced (you need about
   120ml of juice)

To decorate
1 quantity Italian meringue
   (page 27)

I have rarely seen this pairing of lime and chocolate since eating those green and brown boiled sweets when I was younger. I think these pies are a superior format for the flavour pairing! The Key lime pie-inspired filling and chocolate shortcrust pastry contain bitter notes that welcome the sweet meringue topping. I recommend that you don't go overboard with the meringue, or you could be at risk of making the pies overbearingly sweet.

METHOD

Preheat the oven to 180°C fan/ 190°C conventional/gas mark 5.

1. Make and blind bake individual chocolate pastry cases as instructed on page 18. Mine were 10cm pastry cases.

Reduce the oven to 150°C fan/ 160°C conventional/gas mark 3.

Make the filling
1. Whisk together the egg yolks and sugar; then whisk in the condensed milk, double cream and lime zest until combined. Finally, gradually stream in the lime juice, whisking all the time. The mixture will thicken considerably at this stage.

2. Fill the pastry cases with the mixture. Bake for 15 minutes until the centres display a gentle wobble. Out of the oven, carefully remove the tarts from their tins and leave to cool on a wire rack.

Decorate the pies
1. Pipe or spread over the Italian meringue and brown it by passing a blowtorch flame over the meringue. Don't worry if you don't own a blowtorch – this isn't essential.

CARAMEL CHOCOLATE TART

INGREDIENTS

1 quantity chocolate sweet
   shortcrust pastry
   (page 18) (gf)

For the filling
1 quantity salted caramel
   sauce (page 34)
   (high butter and low
   cream content)
280g double cream
200g dark chocolate
20g butter
Flaky sea salt

I do consider balance in most of my recipes. Combining sweetness with something bitter or creaminess with something sharp is typically a sensible thing to do when creating a recipe. But balance has not been considered here. I thought I'd go all-in for this bake! It does what it says on the tin; this is a chocolate pastry case filled with caramel and chocolate ganache, nothing fancy about it, just pure indulgence. Each bite is incredibly rich and wonderfully satisfying. I will warn you, though, it's best to take a very thin slice and finish wanting more. It's quite easy to scupper yourself on this one.

METHOD

Preheat the oven to 180°C fan/ 190°C conventional/gas mark 5.

1. Blind bake a 20–23cm chocolate shortcrust pastry case as instructed on page 18. Leave to cool.

Make the filling
1. Make a salted caramel sauce as instructed on page 34, with additional butter and reduced cream. Leave this to cool for about 15 minutes at room temperature, then pour about three quarters of it into the tart case. Leave to chill in the fridge.

2. Heat the double cream in a pan until just bubbling. Add in the chocolate and gently stir until you achieve a smooth texture. Add in the butter and stir to combine. Pour this mixture over the caramel and leave it to set in the fridge for at least 2 hours.

3. Sprinkle some flaky sea salt over the tart and serve in thin slices.

How to serve
1. It is best to slice this tart fridge-cold with a warm knife, but then serve and eat the tart at room temperature, so the filling is soft and silky.

NEAPOLITAN NAPOLEON

INGREDIENTS

1 quantity rough puff pastry
    (page 14) (gf)
Icing sugar, to sieve

**For the vanilla crème
    légère**
100ml milk
1 large egg yolk
25g caster sugar
10g cornflour
1½ teaspoons vanilla bean
    paste
100ml double cream
10g icing sugar

**For the chocolate
    ganache**
100g double cream
100g milk chocolate

To assemble
100g strawberry jam
50g icing sugar
Strawberries, sliced to
    decorate

This bake combines 3 layers of rough puff pastry sandwiched with 2 layers of crème légère, ganache and jam. A bake of this style is often called a mille-feuille or Napoleon. Some say there are minor differences between the 2 pastries; however, I'm calling this bake a Napoleon purely for the sake of alliteration. It's firmly inspired by memories of eating tubs of Neapolitan ice cream with those distinctive strawberry, chocolate and vanilla stripes. I can confidently say that this is a more refined iteration of the classic flavour pairing, although it would still appeal to my childhood cravings!

METHOD

Preheat the oven to 200°C fan/ 210°C conventional/gas mark 7.

Bake the pastry

1. Cut your pastry in half. Roll each half into a rectangle approximately 32cm x 15cm and just under ½ cm thick. Place each rectangle of pastry onto a lined baking tray.

2. Liberally dust each sheet of pastry by sieving over icing sugar, covering it completely. Cover each sheet of pastry with a further sheet of baking paper and top with another baking tray to weigh down the pastry.

3. Bake covered for 20 minutes, then uncover and bake for a further 5 to 10 minutes or until deeply golden. Leave to cool.

4. Use a sharp knife to slice each sheet of pastry into 9 rectangles measuring 9cm x 4cm.

Make the vanilla crème légère

1. See page 47 for instructions and use the quantities listed for this recipe.

2. Fill a piping bag with the crème and leave in the fridge until it needs to be used.

Make the chocolate ganache

1. Heat the double cream in a pan until just bubbling. Add in the chocolate and stir until smooth and combined.

2. Set the ganache aside to cool to room temperature, so that it is thick enough to hold its shape. This can take a couple of hours or can be sped up in the fridge.

3. Fill a piping bag with the thickened ganache.

Assemble the Napoleon

1. Lay down a rectangle of pastry. Pipe on 4 to 5 alternating dots of chocolate ganache and crème légère running down both sides of the pastry. Fill a piping bag with the jam and pipe a line down the middle of the crème and ganache. Do this for each of 12 rectangles.

2. Gently lay one piped rectangle over another, so there are 6 double layers.

3. Dust the remaining 6 pastry rectangles with icing sugar and top with a dod of crème and a slice of strawberry.

CINNAMON SWIRLS

INGREDIENTS

Leftover rough puff pastry
    (gf)
20g butter, melted
75g demerara sugar
1 teaspoon cinnamon

Cinnamon swirls are nothing more than a simpler way to shape a classic little French pastry called a *palmier*. A *palmier* is rolled from both sides into the centre resulting in a shape like an elephant's ear – or a palm leaf. No matter how you roll the pastry, it is still sweet, cinnamony, flaky and delicious.

For me, this recipe is a go-to when it comes to using up leftover rough puff pastry. You can make a very small batch or a massive batch depending on how much pastry is going spare. In theory, these will keep well in an airtight container for a long time. However, I can't tell you how long this would be as they have always been eaten up well before day two!

METHOD

Preheat the oven to 190°C fan/ 200°C conventional/gas mark 6. Line a baking tray.

1. Roll out the pastry on a lightly floured surface into a rough rectangle about 2 times longer than it is wide.

2. Brush the pastry with the melted butter. Mix together the sugar and cinnamon and generously sprinkle this over the pastry in an even layer.

3. Tack the close side of the pastry down onto your worktop. Start from the other side and roll it up tightly into a swirl, making sure the bottom edge of pastry is tacked down to the roll. Roll from the short side if you want big pastries or the long side if you want small pastries. Chill in the fridge for at least 20 minutes.

4. Cut slices about ½ cm thick from the roll of dough. Bake for 15 to 20 minutes or until golden and crunchy.

LEFTOVER PASTRY TURNOVERS

INGREDIENTS

Leftover shortcrust or rough
    puff pastry (gf)
1 teaspoon jam, curd or
    spread of your choice
    (per turnover)
1 egg, beaten
30g demerara sugar

There is nothing mind-blowing about this bake, but it's useful to have a couple of ideas to help use up leftover pastry. It's rare that I don't have a little ball of excess pastry after making a tart or pie. Particularly when you've spent the time and effort to make the pastry from scratch, you don't want to see it go to waste, so bake away, and you get to enjoy a tasty teatime treat while cutting down on your food waste. Typically, I would use jam or curd for fillings, but you can use anything you like. Caramel sauce, chocolate ganache or spread, peanut butter and many more would all work.

METHOD

Preheat the oven to 190°C fan/
200°C conventional/gas mark 6.

1. Roll the pastry to a little under
    ½ cm thick. Cut circles from the
    dough that are about 8cm to
    10cm in diameter.

2. Fill each circle of dough with a
    small teaspoon of the filling of
    your choice in the centre. If you
    overfill the pastries, they will split
    open in the oven. Brush the edge
    of one half of the dough with egg
    wash. Fold the pastry over and
    press down firmly. Use a slightly
    smaller cutter to cut away a tiny
    portion of the pastry edge to seal
    the two sides together.

3. Brush the top of the pastry with
    egg wash and sprinkle with
    demerara sugar. Bake for 15 to
    20 minutes or until deeply golden.

PECAN AND WALNUT PIE

INGREDIENTS

1 quantity sweet shortcrust
    pastry (page 18) (gf)
125g pecans
125g walnuts
80g butter, melted
100g dark brown sugar
75g golden syrup
75g maple syrup
80ml double cream
1 tablespoon cornflour
2 large eggs, beaten
1 teaspoon vanilla bean
    paste
½ teaspoon salt

My flatmate, Abhi, describes pecans as 'the king of the nuts', and even he is in favour of the addition of its cousin, the walnut, in this pie. Pecans are objectively delicious with their sweet butteriness, so the addition of walnuts isn't to cover up the pecans, it's just to add another layer of interest. Walnuts bring a different flavour profile with their slight acidity and bitterness, plus a texture that is a little waxier and softer. Roasting the nuts first is key to making this pie delicious. The flavour is really bolstered by this step, so be sure not to skip it.

METHOD

Preheat the oven to 180°C fan/
190°C conventional/gas mark 5.

1. Blind bake a 20–23cm pastry
   case as instructed on page 18.

2. Roast the pecans and walnuts
   for 7 to 10 minutes until slightly
   darkened and smelling roasty and
   nutty.

Reduce the oven to 160°C fan/
170°C conventional/gas mark 3.5.

1. Roughly chop half of the roasted
   nuts and spread these over the
   pastry case.

2. Whisk together the butter, sugar
   and syrups until smooth. Whisk
   through the cream, cornflour,
   eggs, vanilla and salt until
   combined.

3. Pour this mixture over the chopped
   nuts in the pastry case leaving at
   least ½ cm of space to the top of
   the pastry case. Cover the filling
   with the remaining whole nuts and
   fill up to just below the rim of the
   pastry case with any more filling
   (you may not need to use it all for
   a smaller tart). Bake for about 40
   minutes, until the filling around
   the nuts appears set with a gentle
   quiver in the middle.

4. Remove from the tin and cool on a
   wire rack.

TREACLE TART

INGREDIENTS

1 quantity sweet shortcrust
    pastry (page 18) (gf)
400g golden syrup
30g butter
1 lemon, zested and juiced
2 tablespoons double cream
150g brown breadcrumbs
    (gf) (easiest to whizz
    bread in a food
    processor)
1 large egg, beaten
½ teaspoon salt

Treacle tart is stodgy, comforting and warming. It's delicious eaten cold but even better served warm with a big scoop of vanilla ice cream. The lemon in the filling adds a bit of zip and zing to balance what is otherwise an incredibly sweet bake; a good amount of salt also aids this goal. The result is still very sweet and best served in reasonably thin slices. It's one of those desserts that it's better to finish wanting more rather than feeling the consequences of indulging too much!

METHOD

Preheat the oven to 180°C fan/ 190°C conventional/gas mark 5.

1. Blind bake a 20–23cm pastry case as instructed on page 18.

Reduce the oven to 160°C fan/ 170°C conventional/gas mark 3.5.

1. Heat the golden syrup and butter gently in a pan until the butter has just melted.

2. Remove from the heat and stir through the lemon juice, zest and double cream. Add in the breadcrumbs and stir through along with the egg and salt until combined.

3. Pour the filling into the pastry, so it sits just below the top of the case. You may not need to use all the filling if you are making a smaller tart. Bake for about 35 minutes, until the filling looks set with a slight quiver.

4. Remove from the tin and leave to cool on a wire rack.

CHAPTER 4
PUDDINGS

I believe puddings can be distinguished from desserts. A pudding, for me, is what my mum might rustle up on a Wednesday night when we were kids and serve with lashings of bright yellow custard. Puddings are simple to make, comforting, often warming and frequently stodgy (which is, in my considered opinion, the best texture!).

STICKY TOFFEE PUDDING

INGREDIENTS

150g dates, chopped
1 teaspoon vanilla bean
    paste
1 teaspoon instant coffee
    powder
½ teaspoon bicarbonate
    of soda
½ teaspoon salt
150ml water, boiling
75g butter, softened
115g dark brown sugar
2 large eggs
125g self-raising flour (gf)
75g walnuts, chopped

To serve
1 to 2 quantities caramel
    sauce (page 34)

STP is my desert island dessert, my all-time favourite, the undisputed champ of puddings! It has some tough competition, but I don't think anything can beat a good STP. My number one issue if I have this when out for dinner is that it's rarely served with enough toffee sauce. I eat my STP by mashing down each spoonful into the toffee sauce so that each taste is saturated with toffee goodness. Weird, but just so good!

My bizarre technique clearly requires a healthy portion of sauce and is probably why I frequently run low on toffee sauce out at a restaurant. I wouldn't want you to struggle with the same issue at home, so I recommend making a double batch of caramel sauce (see page 34). Worst case scenario is that there's some leftover caramel sauce to enjoy with ice cream tomorrow. It doesn't sound like a bad situation to me!

METHOD

Preheat the oven to 170°C fan/ 180°C conventional/gas mark 4. Grease 6 dariole moulds with butter and line the base with a small circle of baking paper.

1. Add the dates, vanilla, coffee, bicarbonate of soda and salt into a bowl and cover with the boiling water. Leave aside to soak for 15 to 30 minutes.

2. Cream the butter and sugar until light and fluffy. Mix through the eggs and flour, followed by gradually mixing through the date mixture with its liquid and the walnuts. It doesn't matter if the batter becomes a little split.

3. Fill the moulds two thirds full. Bake in the oven for 20 to 25 minutes until a skewer comes out clean.

4. Allow to cool for about 5 minutes before turning out from the moulds. If they are a little stuck, run a knife around the mould to release the puddings. Serve hot with lashings of warm caramel sauce and ice cream!

STEAMED SYRUP PUDDING

INGREDIENTS

100g golden syrup
150g butter, softened
100g light brown sugar
½ teaspoon salt
1 lemon, zested
3 large eggs
150g self-raising flour (gf)
1 teaspoon baking powder
    (gf)

Magic happens when you steam a sponge. You can't get the same texture from any other method. It's incredibly moist, quite light textured, but also has that very satisfying mouth feel I usually associate with dense stodgy things; this isn't dense, though. It tastes great cold, but its natural home is served hot with loads of yellow shop-bought custard or just as much of the classier homemade stuff (see page 45).

METHOD

Thoroughly grease a 1 litre or 2 pint pudding basin. Line the base with a circle of baking paper.

1. Pour 50g of golden syrup into the base of the pudding basin.

2. Add the remaining golden syrup into a bowl with the butter and sugar. Cream together with an electric mixer until light and fluffy; this will take about 3 to 5 minutes. Add all the remaining ingredients and stir until combined.

3. Add the mixture into the pudding basin and level off. If using a plastic pudding basin, grease the inside of the lid and clip into place. If not, cut a circle of baking paper and foil about 10cm larger in diameter than the basin. Place the baking paper over the basin and cover with the foil, then tuck around the basin. Tie the foil around the basin with string. Fold a sheet of foil 4 times lengthways to create a long, strong piece of foil. Place the pudding basin onto the middle of this foil strip, using it as a handle.

4. Place a small, upturned plate into the base of a large pan. Sit the pudding basin on the plate and fill around with boiling water reaching about 2cm up the side of the basin. Place a lid on the pan and gently simmer on a low heat, allowing the pudding to steam for about 90 minutes. Check the water level periodically to make sure the pan does not run dry. Check the sponge is cooked by pressing a skewer into the centre; it should come out clean.

5. Leave the pudding to cool for about 5 minutes before placing your serving plate over the pudding and inverting it to turn out. Optionally, you can drizzle additional golden syrup over the pudding to give it a shine.

6. Serve with lashings of pouring cream, custard (page 45), ice cream (page 50) or clotted cream.

BROWN SUGAR RICE PUDDING WITH STEWED APPLES

INGREDIENTS

For the rice pudding

40g butter

85g arborio or pudding rice

50g dark brown sugar

1 litre oat milk (can substitute
for other milk or milk
alternative) (gf oat milk is
available)

35g porridge oats (gf)

½ teaspoon cinnamon

½ teaspoon salt

For the toppings

1 large cooking apple

60g light brown sugar

½ lemon, juiced

50ml apple juice (or water)

½ teaspoon cinnamon

2 medium eating apples

1 quantity oaty crumble
(page 48) (gf)

This is not much of a looker. The aesthetic is clearly 'brown'. There's nothing wrong with a comforting brown pud, though, and we've not shied away from it here. The beautiful brown is accentuated with the addition of oat milk, brown butter and brown sugar. They don't just add to the colour; the dish is centred around nutty, caramelly flavours, which, when combined with a good hit of salt, leads this dish to make me say 'phwah, yeah' when tucking in!

This recipe is very much about loose guidelines, not strict rules and ratios. Feel free to switch out the oat milk for a different milk (standard or alternative); you can switch out the oats for additional rice (they are there to give a thick creamy texture); you can change the type of sugar or flavourings, and you can top it with whatever you want.

METHOD

Preheat the oven to 140°C fan/
150°C conventional/gas mark 2.

Make the rice pudding

1. Place the butter in a large saucepan over a high heat. Stir occasionally as the butter foams. Once the bubbles subside, it should look brown and smell toasty. Remove the pan from the heat and stir in the pudding rice for about a minute.

2. Place the pan back on a medium heat and stir in the sugar and oat milk. Bring to the boil, reduce to a simmer and add in the oats, cinnamon and salt. Simmer for about 5 minutes, then transfer into a large dish (about 1.5 litres).

3. Bake for 30 minutes. Remove from the oven, stir and place back in for an additional 45 to 75 minutes. It will form a skin on top. Taste a small portion of rice from under the skin to ensure it is tender and cooked through. If the rice still has a bite, put it back in the oven for an extra 15 minutes, checking until cooked.

Make the toppings

1. Peel, core and small dice the cooking apple. Place in a saucepan with the sugar, lemon and apple juice and cinnamon over a medium-low heat. Cook for about 5 minutes, occasionally stirring until the apples begin to break down.

2. Peel, core and dice the eating apples. Add them to the pan with the cooking apples, stir occasionally and cook for about 10 to 15 minutes until the apples are beginning to soften but retain a good bite. The cooking apples should be almost completely broken down.

3. If the mixture has a little too much liquid, simmer until it is the thickness you desire.

4. Serve the rice pudding hot alongside warm stewed apples and the oaty crumble.

LEMON AND BLACKBERRY BREAD AND BUTTER PUDDING

INGREDIENTS

300g shop-bought brioche
    (loaf or rolls) (gf)
150g lemon curd (page 41)
150g blackberries
4 large egg yolks,
    plus 1 large egg
75g sugar
1 lemon, zested and juiced
300ml whole milk
200ml double cream
30g butter, for greasing

Pillowy soft, lemon zingy brioche covers a hidden layer of comforting silky, creamy custard when you dig into this pudding. When I tested this recipe, the review from Jamie my flatmate was simply a collection of contented, happy, yummy noises!

Brioche is already enriched with butter and eggs, so it adds another layer of luxury to the experience and means you can get away without buttering the bread. So, I've switched out bread-buttering – with its inevitable bread-tearing butter drags – for the much easier act of lemon-'curding' the brioche. (I don't think that term will catch on.) This balances a decadent treat with just enough zing, and I hope it will leave you wanting to come back for more.

METHOD

Preheat the oven to 170°C fan/ 180°C conventional/gas mark 4. Grease a 1.5 litre oven-safe dish with butter.

1. Slice the brioche loaf into about 8 thick slices, or split each roll in half. Spread lemon curd over each piece and cut the slices in half into triangles. Tightly pack the lemon curd-covered brioche into the dish. Press the blackberries into any gaps in between.

2. Whisk the eggs with the sugar and lemon juice. Heat the milk and cream with the lemon zest in a pan until beginning to bubble. Gradually whisk the hot milk and cream into the egg mixture.

3. Pour the custard over the brioche. Leave aside to soak for 20 to 30 minutes. It will look like too much liquid to start with, but will soak in when given time.

4. Bake in the oven for 25 to 30 minutes. The top should appear almost set, with a liquid custard underneath. Leave to cool briefly for about 5 minutes before serving.

APPLE AND PLUM COBBLER

INGREDIENTS

For the fruit

600g plums, stoned

400g eating apples, peeled
and cored

100g light brown sugar

1 lemon, zested and juiced

1 teaspoon ground
cinnamon

15g cornflour, plus
2 teaspoon water

For the cobbler dough

125g butter, cubed

200g self-raising flour (gf)

75g ground almonds

½ teaspoon salt

½ teaspoon baking powder
(gf)

½ teaspoon ground
cinnamon

40g caster sugar

40g light brown sugar

1 large egg

75ml milk

30g demerara sugar

My reference point for cobbler comes from my mum's gooseberry cobbler. Topping stewed fruit with a light scone-like batter is a nice change from the equally delicious crumble if you have a glut of fruit that needs using and you're running out of ideas. When I was very little, I remember working around the sharp gooseberries and going straight for the sweet cobbler and lashings of custard. Now I appreciate a good gooseberry pud, but I used to find it somewhat challenging. The combo of apple and plum in this cobbler is certainly not challenging! Sweet soft fruit gently spiced with cinnamon is pretty much a dead-cert for anyone who likes stewed fruit. The great thing about the structure of a cobbler is that you can so easily change up the filling to whatever fruit is lying around and beginning to turn a little past its best.

METHOD

Preheat the oven to 170°C fan/ 180°C conventional/gas mark 4.

Prepare the fruit

1. Roughly chop the plums and apples into a medium dice. Lay these into a large ovenproof dish. Stir through the sugar, lemon zest and juice and cinnamon. Leave to sit for 15 to 30 minutes, allowing some of the juices to release from the fruit. Mix the cornflour with water into a slurry and stir into the fruit mixture. Bake for about 15 minutes while you prepare the cobbler topping.

Make the cobbler

1. Rub the cubed butter into the flour until it resembles breadcrumbs; it doesn't matter if there are a few lumps of butter still present. Stir through the ground almonds, salt, baking powder, cinnamon, caster sugar and brown sugar. Add in the egg and milk, stirring with a table knife to create a rough dough that resembles a very soft scone dough.

2. Take the fruit out of the oven and cover the mixture with about 6 or 7 large spoonfuls of the cobbler mix. It's fine to leave a few gaps showing the fruit underneath.

3. Sprinkle demerara sugar over the cobbler mix. Bake for about 40 minutes, or until the top of the cobbler is golden and brown. Serve hot with cream, ice cream or custard.

BERRY AND APPLE CRUMBLE

INGREDIENTS

For the filling
400g eating apples, peeled
    and cored
500g frozen mixed berries,
    or a mix of fresh berries
100g sugar
15g cornflour, plus
    2 teaspoons water

For the crumble topping
200g plain flour (gf)
150g butter, cubed (cold or
    softened)
75g porridge oats (gf)
100g demerara sugar
1 teaspoon salt
75g flaked almonds
    (optional)

Surely the number one comfort dessert ('and don't call me, Shirley'). The biggest topic for debate in the crumble world has to be the ratio of fruit to crumble. As I've grown up, I have noticed a shift in my optimum ratio leaning towards the fruit more and more – maybe that's just me trying to be fancy? I'm happy with the ratio I've obtained in this recipe; it results in a good amount of sharp and sweet fruit, a soggy layer of fruit-soaked crumble, along with a crisp topping. The most important part for me is the soggy, soaked layer of crumble. That part brings the stodge. Stodge is synonymous with comfort in my mind, and comfort is what a crumble is all about.

METHOD

Preheat the oven to 170°C fan/
180°C conventional/gas mark 4.

Make the filling
1. Chop the apples into approximately 2cm cubes. Add to a pan along with the berries and sugar. Cook over a high heat for about 5 minutes until the berries have released their juices. Stir together the cornflour and water into a slurry. Stir this into the fruit and cook for a couple of minutes until thickened. Pour the fruit into an ovenproof dish.

Make the crumble topping
1. Rub the butter into the flour until it looks like rough breadcrumbs. It's fine for it to be quite rough and for fairly big lumps of butter to remain. Stir through the oats, sugar, salt and almonds.

2. Press some of the crumble mixture together with your hands to form clumps as you sprinkle it over the fruit, covering the fruit completely.

3. Bake in the oven for about 40 minutes or until the top is enticingly golden with some pools of jammy juice peeking through. Serve hot with ice cream, custard or cream . . . or all three!

PIÑA COLADA TRIFLE

INGREDIENTS

For the Swiss roll
4 large eggs
110g caster sugar
1 teaspoon vanilla bean
    paste
110g self-raising flour (gf)
20g desiccated coconut

For the pineapple curd
150ml pineapple juice
1 lime, zested and juiced
60g caster sugar
4 large egg yolks
70g unsalted butter, cubed

**For the roasted
    pineapple**
1 large pineapple, peeled
    and cored (reserve the
    leaves for decoration)
80g light brown sugar

For the coconut custard
3 x 400g tins coconut milk
5 large eggs, plus 3 large
    egg yolks
75g caster sugar
30g cornflour

**For the pineapple jelly
    (optional)**
4 sheets leaf gelatine
    (any grade)
400ml pineapple juice
100ml coconut rum

For the rum soak
75ml white or coconut rum
75ml pineapple juice

For the whipped cream
300ml double cream
30g icing sugar

This isn't a particularly classy bake, but it is definitely fun, and surely that's the point of a trifle. Trifle is a retro party centrepiece. It should make you go wow, and maybe giggle when you see the whole creation in its bowl, but it doesn't have to (and it won't) look good on a plate when served. It should become a mess of soft sponge, creamy custard and sweet jelly, and with all the textures mixing and mingling together is how it should be eaten. There are many different elements to a trifle, which means it actually takes quite a while to put together, so feel free to cheat on any stage with shop-bought alternatives.

METHOD

Preheat the oven to 170°C fan/ 180°C conventional/gas mark 4. Grease and line a Swiss roll tin, about 33cm x 23cm.

Make the Swiss roll
1. Make and bake a Swiss roll sponge as instructed on page 24. Sprinkle the desiccated coconut over the sponge before baking.

2. Roll the cake while warm and unroll, leaving it to cool.

Make the pineapple curd
1. Heat the pineapple juice in a pan over a high heat until it has reduced by about half. Measure out the juice, add in the lime juice making the volume up to 90ml.

2. Use this mixture and the remaining ingredients to make the curd as instructed on page 41. Cool in the fridge.

3. Once the curd has cooled, spread it in an even layer over the Swiss roll sponge. Use the bottom sheet of baking paper to roll up the Swiss roll into a tight spiral from the short side. Slice 1.5cm-thick slices from the roll.

Increase the oven to 190°C fan/ 200°C conventional/gas mark 6.

Roast the pineapple
1. Chop half of the pineapple into roughly 2cm cubes. Cut the remaining half into rings ½ cm thick and cut in half to create pineapple semicircles. Place these in a rimmed baking tray and toss through the sugar.

2. Roast for 20 to 30 minutes, stirring every 10 minutes until the pineapple is covered in a sticky, golden coating. Set aside to cool in the fridge.

Make the coconut custard
1. Heat the coconut milk in a non-stick pan until it begins to bubble.

2. Whisk the eggs and yolks with the sugar, whisk through the cornflour.

3. Pour the hot coconut milk over the egg mixture, stirring constantly. Return this mixture to the pan and cook over a high heat until bubbling and thickened, stirring constantly. Pour into a clean bowl or shallow tray and cover the surface with cling film or baking paper and leave to chill in the fridge.

Continues overleaf . . .

PIÑA COLADA TRIFLE
CONTINUED

For decoration
30g toasted coconut flakes
20g maraschino cherries
Pineapple leaves
Cocktail umbrellas

Make the pineapple jelly

1. Soak the gelatine in cold water for about 5 minutes.

2. Heat up 100ml of pineapple juice until just beginning to steam from the surface. Remove from the heat, squeeze out the excess liquid from the gelatine and stir into the warm juice to melt. Add in the remaining cold juice and coconut rum, then stir to combine.

Make the rum soak

1. Mix together the rum with the pineapple juice.

Assemble the trifle

1. Dunk one side of the Swiss roll slices into the rum soak and press into the side of your trifle bowl to create a circle all the way around the bowl. Lay any remaining cake slices over the bottom of the bowl and sprinkle any remaining soak over the sponges.

2. Give the custard a quick beat to smooth it out, then use it to fill the base of the dish up to the level of the top of the Swiss rolls. This should use a little under half of the custard.

3. Press the pineapple semicircles against the glass all the way around the bowl. Lay the roasted pineapple chunks over the custard in a single layer. Very gently pour the room-temperature jelly over the pineapple chunks. You need to pour it slowly, so it doesn't break through the custard. Place this back in the fridge for about an hour or until the jelly has set.

4. Pour the remaining portion of custard over the set jelly and level off. Place back in the fridge until nearly ready to serve.

5. Before serving, whip the cream with the icing sugar to medium peaks. Spread this over the custard.

6. Top the trifle with toasted coconut flakes, maraschino cherries, pineapple leaves and cocktail umbrellas!

MANGO AND PASSIONFRUIT CHEESECAKE

INGREDIENTS

For the biscuit base

250g bourbon biscuits (or gf chocolate sandwich biscuit alternative)

110g butter, melted

For the cheesecake filling

400g tinned mango pulp or 200g thick mango purée (page 40)

200ml double cream

110g icing sugar

350g cream cheese

For the passionfruit jelly

1½ sheets leaf gelatine (any grade)

4 passionfruit

125ml tropical fruit juice (or a diluted cordial if you prefer)

Mango blends so well into a creamy cheesecake filling. The passionfruit jelly layer brings that bit of zip and zing to the party, which I really like. This recipe doesn't have many ingredients for a bake with three different layers, each with different textures and flavours. Each component is straightforward to make, so it can be a very relaxing and stress-free experience if you just allow enough time for chilling in between the easy stages.

METHOD

Preheat the oven to 170°C fan/180°C conventional/gas mark 4. You need a 20cm loose-based deep cake tin.

Make the biscuit base

1. Blitz the biscuits in a food processor, or smash in a bag with a rolling pin to a fine crumb. Add to a bowl and stir through the melted butter. Pour this into your tin. Use the back of a spoon to press it tightly into the tin. Bake for 10 minutes, on a baking tray to catch melting butter, then remove and leave to cool in the tin. The base may puff up a little during baking. If this happens, press it down flat with a spoon while warm.

Make the cheesecake filling

1. Place the mango pulp or purée into a non-stick pan over a high heat. Stir frequently and boil away until it reduces by half, is thick and weighs about 200g. Chill this to fridge cold.

2. Whisk the double cream and 60g of icing sugar to medium-stiff peaks. In a separate bowl, beat together the cream cheese, cooled mango pulp and remaining 50g of icing sugar until just combined. Fold the whipped cream through the mango cream cheese mixture until smooth and all one colour.

3. Pour the mango filling onto the biscuit base and level off flat with a small offset spatula or spoon. Place in the fridge to chill for at least 2 hours.

Make the passionfruit jelly

1. Soak the gelatine sheets in cold water for about 5 minutes until softened.

2. Scoop out the passionfruit seeds into a sieve. Press the seeds with the back of a spoon to release the juice through the sieve. Reserve the seeds.

3. Measure out the passionfruit juice and add the additional tropical juice, so the total volume is 175ml.

4. Pour 50ml of the juice into a pan and heat until the liquid is steaming, not quite bubbling, then remove the pan from the heat. Squeeze out any excess liquid from the gelatine and add this into the warm juice; stir until the gelatine has dissolved. Stir in the remaining cold juice and about a quarter of the reserved passionfruit seeds.

Continues overleaf . . .

MANGO AND PASSIONFRUIT CHEESECAKE CONTINUED

5. Leave the jelly to cool in the fridge until a little cool to the touch but still fluid. This should take about 5 to 15 minutes. Don't leave it too long, or it will set. If it sets, gently warm it up in a pan until liquid again.

6. Gently pour the cool jelly over the cold cheesecake filling, ensuring the seeds are well dispersed through the jelly topping. Place in the fridge for at least an hour or until the jelly has set.

7. Carefully remove from the tin by sitting the tin on a tall glass or jar and gently pressing down on the outside of the tin. If the cheesecake gets stuck, gently warm the outside of the tin with a blowtorch or warm damp cloth.

8. Decorate with your remaining passionfruit seeds.

RHUBARB AND ORANGE PUDDINGS

INGREDIENTS

For the rhubarb

300g rhubarb
70g sugar
3 tablespoons Cointreau
    (or orange juice)
10g cornflour

For the sponge

180g butter, softened
150g caster sugar
2 large eggs, plus 1 large
    yolk
2 oranges, zested and
    juiced
120g self-raising flour (gf)
120g ground almonds
½ teaspoon baking powder
    (gf)
½ teaspoon salt

This recipe wasn't in my original plan for this book. However, when rhubarb season came around and I got my hands on some beautiful vibrant forced rhubarb, I was inspired to bake more with it. This is my favourite way to create a bake, starting with an amazing raw product and writing the recipe around that to celebrate it.

It is really simple to put this together. The combination of sharp rhubarb against sweet orange and almond works so well. The cake is delicious eaten cold, the sponge has a satisfyingly firm texture, and the cool rhubarb zings. When served warm, the sponge turns meltingly tender and soft and screams out to be draped in custard (see page 45).

METHOD

Preheat the oven to 190°C fan/ 200°C conventional/gas mark 6. Grease 6 dariole moulds with butter and line the bases with a circle of baking paper.

Roast the rhubarb

1. Cut half the rhubarb (150g) into roughly 4cm lengths. Lay these in a rimmed baking tray and sprinkle over 20g of sugar.

2. Roast for about 10 minutes until softened but holding its shape.

3. Set the rhubarb aside to cool.

Reduce the oven to 160°C fan/ 170°C conventional/gas mark 3.

Make the stewed rhubarb filling

1. Chop the remaining 150g of rhubarb. Place in a pan with the 50g of sugar and Cointreau over a medium heat. Bring to the boil, reduce the heat and simmer for 5 minutes, so the fruit is breaking down.

2. Mix the cornflour into a slurry with about 2 teaspoons of cold water and add to the rhubarb.

3. Stir over a medium heat until thickened. Leave aside to cool.

Make the sponge

1. Cream the butter and sugar until light and fluffy; this will take about 5 minutes.

2. Add in the remaining ingredients and mix until just combined. Fill a piping bag with this mixture.

Assemble and bake

1. Place a piece or two of roasted rhubarb into the bottom of each dariole mould.

2. Pipe the sponge over and around the rhubarb and up the sides of the mould, leaving a cavity in the middle.

3. Place a spoonful of the rhubarb into the cavity, top with a little more sponge and smooth out with the back of a teaspoon to cover the rhubarb. It's okay if you can see some rhubarb poking through.

4. Bake for about 25 minutes until golden, and the sponge appears set when gently pressed.

5. Leave to cool in the tins for about 5 minutes before removing. If the cakes get stuck, run a knife around the outside of the moulds to help them release.

QUICK CHOCOLATE AND HAZELNUT MOUSSE

INGREDIENTS

250ml double cream
25g icing sugar
250g chocolate hazelnut
    spread
30g roasted hazelnuts, for
    decoration

This mousse was a happy accident. I aimed to make a creamy chocolate filling or frosting for a cupcake, but after tasting this mix, I realised it was good enough to eat on its own, so I gave it its own recipe. Three minutes would be a high estimation for how long this pudding takes to make; I reckon you could drill it down to under two. But it doesn't matter that it takes such little time and little effort; I would happily serve it at any casual family meal or, equally, a 'get the fancy china out' dinner party.

When freshly made, it has a light, airy and soft texture; if you leave it in the fridge for a few hours, it firms up and becomes a more thick and unctuous mousse. So, make it ahead, or make it last minute without the concern of neglecting any guests for long while you prepare their delicious pudding. This recipe makes enough for 4.

METHOD

1. Whip the cream with the icing sugar to medium-firm peaks.

2. Add in the chocolate hazelnut spread and whisk through until just combined.

3. Spoon or pipe into your serving dishes and chill in the fridge.

4. Top the mousse with chopped roasted hazelnuts and serve!

NO-CHURN OAT AND RASPBERRY ICE CREAM

INGREDIENTS

For the oat brittle

75g oatmeal or rolled oats
    (gf rolled oats)
100g caster sugar
2 tablespoons water
Pinch of flaky salt

For the ice cream

600ml double cream
40g skimmed milk powder
100g clear honey
1 teaspoon vanilla bean
    paste
4 tablespoons whisky
    (optional)
150g raspberries

This is a stupidly simple and decadent pudding. It is firmly inspired by a Delia Smith recipe my mum made for a dinner party when I was about 7 or 8. She only made it once, but it was so good that I retained a very strong memory of the taste for all these years and knew I had to replicate something similar. The resulting pudding is a super creamy and rich ice cream, with crunchy caramelised oats and fresh raspberries running through.

The ingredients and process involved help keep it soft and creamy without churning. Whipping the cream before freezing adds the lightness that you would achieve in the traditional churning process. Honey acts as a good anti-freeze to prevent the ice cream from setting too hard; this is also aided by the cream's high fat content and the addition of whisky, if you use it. The milk powder adds body by adding solids without any additional water, which would encourage an icy texture to the final product.

METHOD

Line a rimmed baking tray with baking paper.

Make the oat brittle

1. Toast the oatmeal or oats in a dry pan over a medium heat for a couple of minutes until browned and smelling toasty. Remove from the pan.

2. Add the sugar into the pan with the water. Stir together over a high heat until dissolved and bubbling. Stop stirring and leave to bubble away until it turns a deep amber caramel. Add in the toasted oats and flaky salt, briefly mix together, then pour out onto your prepared tray and leave to cool and solidify.

3. Once solidified, break up into small pieces in a pestle and mortar or smash in a bag with a rolling pin. This brittle is too hard for my food processor, so a pestle and mortar is best, followed by the rolling pin method.

Make the ice cream

1. Add the double cream into a large bowl with the milk powder, honey, vanilla and whisky if desired. Whisk to soft-medium peaks. Briefly fold through the oat brittle and raspberries.

2. Pour the mixture into a 900g loaf tin and place in the freezer for at least 4 hours.

3. When ready to serve, dunk the outside of the tin in warm water to melt the edge of the ice cream and turn it out onto a serving tray. Serve the ice cream in slices. Or, if you prefer, you can leave the ice cream in the tin and scoop out individual portions.

CHAPTER 5
DESSERTS

The desserts here are slightly more refined and a
little classier than the puddings; basically, there isn't
any stodge! Puddings are fantastic to share with
friends and family, but this chapter's recipes will
also serve you well if you were looking to show off
just a little at a dinner party.

BLACKBERRY SOUFFLÉ

INGREDIENTS

30g butter, melted and
    cooled (for greasing)
1 teaspoon cornflour
2 large eggs, separated into
    yolks and whites
100g thin-medium
    blackberry purée
    (page 40)
70g caster sugar, plus
    extra for preparing the
    ramekins
20g icing sugar, for dusting

Soufflé is – for me! – the most exciting dessert. The big wow moment of the way it sits proudly above the ramekin is what draws me to order it when out somewhere fancy. Of course, there is jeopardy in this dessert . . . sometimes the soufflé doesn't rise or falls before serving. Try not to knock out too much air when folding the meringue through the custard base. Once the mixture is one consistent colour, stop folding; they should combine easily if at room temperature because they are both soft textured. The soufflé will always fall once it's out of the oven for a few minutes, so you need to make sure you serve it straight away for your guests to enjoy the full majesty of a well-risen soufflé.

METHOD

Preheat the oven to 180°C fan/ 190°C conventional/gas mark 5. Grease 4 ramekins with melted and cooled butter using a pastry brush to brush upward strokes on the inside of the ramekin. Roll caster sugar around the insides of the ramekins so they are covered in a thin layer. Tip out any excess.

1. Whisk the cornflour into the egg yolks. Stir through the blackberry purée and place into a pan over a high heat. Stir constantly until the mixture bubbles and thickens.

2. Remove from the heat, cover the surface with cling film or baking paper and leave to cool to room temperature.

3. Once the blackberry custard reaches room temperature, add the two egg whites into a separate bowl and whisk to a cloud-like texture with an electric hand whisk. Add in the sugar one tablespoon at a time, whisking for 2 to 3 minutes until the meringue is shiny and holds its peaks but is light and soft.

4. Add one third of the meringue into the blackberry custard and fold in until fully combined and a single smooth colour. Add in the remaining two thirds of the meringue and gently fold in with a flexible spatula until fully combined. Try to do this gently, so you retain as much air as possible in the batter.

5. Fill each of the ramekins with the mixture. Use a palette knife to spread off any excess, so that it's completely level. Run your thumb around the inside rim of the ramekin, leaving an indentation around the top edge of the soufflé.

6. Bake for 14 to 18 minutes or until golden on top; it should be well risen above the ramekin and jiggle gently when tapped. Dust with icing sugar before serving as soon as possible.

RASPBERRY AND VANILLA PANNA COTTA

INGREDIENTS

150g thick raspberry purée
    (page 40)
3½ sheets leaf gelatine
    (any grade)
300ml whole milk
30g caster sugar
2 teaspoons vanilla bean
    paste
300ml double cream

Panna cotta is rich, creamy and unbelievably simple. The addition of a fluid fruit purée centre is a surprise. It adds a layer of complexity to the process, but it's worth it for the hit of the vibrant, punchy fruit centre after you see the plain white exterior flecked with vanilla. Each spoonful melts in your mouth to a cold sweet cream, making it incredibly moreish.

METHOD

1. Fill 6 mini hemisphere silicone moulds with raspberry purée and freeze until solid.

2. Soak the gelatine leaves in cold water for about 5 minutes.

3. Heat the milk and sugar over a medium heat until the sugar has dissolved and the mixture just begins to steam. Take off the heat, squeeze the liquid out of the gelatine and stir into the warm milk to melt.

4. Stir through the vanilla and cold double cream.

5. Fill 6 dariole moulds a third full with the panna cotta mixture. Place in the fridge for about an hour to set. Leave the remaining panna cotta mix at room temperature, so it remains fluid.

6. Press a frozen raspberry purée hemisphere into each panna cotta. Press it slightly into the set mixture, so it is a little fixed. Cover with the remaining panna cotta mixture and place in the fridge to set (this will take between 1 and 2 hours).

7. When you are ready, dunk the moulds in warm water for a couple of seconds to release the panna cotta (you will see it slightly melt around the edges), then invert onto your serving plate

WATERMELON, LIME AND MINT GRANITA

INGREDIENTS

10g fresh mint, finely
   chopped
500g watermelon chunks
2 limes, zested and juiced
75g caster sugar

This dessert is refreshing, clean and bright, and is terrific on a hot summer's night or as a little refresher between courses if you're hosting a super snazzy dinner party. Granita is just a fancy, homemade slushy. You freeze the mixture and periodically break it up with a fork, which creates a snowy texture with individual flakes of frozen sweet watermelon ice. The more frequently you break up the ice, the more delicate the flakes will be and the softer and smoother the result will feel.

METHOD

1. Add the mint, watermelon, lime juice, lime zest and sugar into a food processor or blender. Blitz until liquid.

2. Pour into a shallow tray and put in the freezer for about 45 minutes. Remove from the freezer and mix with a fork to break up the ice crystals as they begin to form around the edges of the tray.

3. Repeat this process until all the mixture is in separated frozen flakes. This should take 3 to 5 repetitions of freezing and breaking up with a fork.

4. Serve in pre-chilled cocktail glasses or bowls.

LEMON PAVLOVA

INGREDIENTS

5 large egg whites
225g caster sugar
175g icing sugar
2 teaspoons cornflour
1 lemon, zested and juiced
300ml double cream
300g lemon curd (page 41)

Icing sugar, cornflour and lemon juice are what gives the pavlova its classic marshmallowy interior. Pavlova can crack very easily and, to be honest, mine often does. The main reason for this is that the sugar is whipped in too quickly, so the meringue gains volume without the sugar dissolving appropriately; the other is that the oven is too hot. It's good to know why these things happen so you can adapt and adjust the next time you bake it, but in the same breath, I don't mind if it cracks and looks very informal; it'll still taste amazing!

METHOD

Preheat the oven to 100°C fan/ 110°C conventional/gas mark ¼. Line a baking tray with non-stick baking paper.

1. Whisk the egg whites on high speed in a stand mixer, or with an electric hand whisk in a large bowl, until they look like light clouds. Mix the caster sugar and 150g of the icing sugar, then gradually add the sugar mixture to the fluffy egg whites while continuing to whisk at medium speed. Add the sugar a heaped dessert spoon at a time, leaving about 20 to 30 seconds between additions.

2. Once all the sugar has been added, the meringue should be very stiff and shiny, and you shouldn't be able to feel any undissolved sugar when rubbing the mix between your fingers. Briefly whisk through the cornflour, lemon zest and 2 teaspoons of lemon juice.

3. Dab a little meringue onto the corners of the baking tray and use this to stick down the baking paper to the tray.

4. Pile the meringue out onto the tray. Use a palette knife to encourage it into a rough circle (or, indeed, any shape you like) of approximately 23cm diameter. Encourage the sides of the pavlova to be tall by spreading up with your palette knife to create ridges.

5. Bake in the oven for about 70 minutes. Once the cooking time is up, turn off the oven and leave the pavlova in there for about 2 hours to cool.

6. Whip the cream with the remaining 25g of icing sugar to soft to medium peaks.

7. Stir the lemon curd to loosen it. Spread about 200g of curd over the pavlova before swooshing the whipped cream over it. Drizzle with more lemon curd and ripple through with a knife.

APPLE MOUSSE CAKE

INGREDIENTS

For the sponge

4 large eggs
110g caster sugar
1 teaspoon vanilla bean
    paste
110g self-raising flour (gf)
1 teaspoon ground
    cinnamon

For the stewed apples

1 large cooking apple
60g light brown sugar
½ lemon, juiced
50ml apple juice
½ teaspoon ground
    cinnamon
2 medium eating apples

For the apple mousse

900ml cloudy apple juice
4 large egg yolks
100g caster sugar
10g cornflour
4 sheets leaf gelatine (any
    grade), soaked in cold
    water for 5 minutes
300ml double cream

To decorate

1 quantity caramel sauce
    (page 34), cooled to
    room temperature
1 eating apple, sliced

A lot of apple juice goes into making this mousse, which gives it a very true apple flavour. The gentle cinnamon spice and caramel apple taste create a lovely autumnal feel as the soft sponge, smooth mousse and firm apples provide great texture. This recipe is reasonably stagey, but each step is straightforward and easy to achieve on its own. Take it step by step and give yourself enough time for chilling, and you'll find the dessert quite simple.

METHOD

Preheat the oven to 170°C fan/ 180°C conventional/gas mark 4. Line a 33cm x 23cm Swiss roll tin with non-stick baking paper.

Make the sponge

1. Make a Swiss roll sponge as instructed on page 24, adding 1 teaspoon of ground cinnamon with the flour. Leave the sponge to cool flat, don't roll it up.

Make the stewed apples

1. Peel, core and small dice the cooking apple. Place in a saucepan with the sugar, lemon juice, apple juice and cinnamon over a medium-low heat. Cook for about 5 minutes, occasionally stirring until the apples are beginning to break down.

2. Peel, core and dice the eating apples. Add them to the pan with the cooking apples, stir occasionally and cook for about 10 to 15 minutes until the apples are beginning to soften but retain a good bite. The cooking apples should be near completely broken down.

3. If the mixture has a little too much liquid, continue to simmer until it has a jammy consistency. Leave to cool in the fridge.

Make the apple mousse

1. Place the apple juice into a non-stick pan and boil until reduced by over a half and measures out to 400ml.

2. Whisk together the egg yolks and sugar, then whisk in the cornflour. Gradually pour in the hot apple juice whisking constantly. Return to the pan and cook over a high heat, continually stirring until boiling and thickened.

3. Once thickened, remove from the heat, squeeze out the excess water from the gelatine and stir into the warm custard to melt. Pour into a bowl, cover the surface with cling film or baking paper and leave to cool to room temperature.

4. Whisk the cream to medium-firm peaks.

5. Whisk the room temperature apple custard to ensure it is smooth. Gently fold the whipped cream through the custard until smooth and all one colour.

Continues overleaf . . .

APPLE MOUSSE CAKE CONTINUED

Assemble the cake

1. Use a 23cm round cake ring or loose-bottomed cake tin to cut a circle from the sponge. Place this onto your serving dish with the cake ring around it if using a ring.

2. Spread the stewed apples over the sponge, leaving a 2cm gap of sponge around the perimeter.

3. Pour the mousse over the apples and sponge. Gently tap down to level off the mousse. Place in the fridge to chill for at least 2 hours or until the mousse has set.

4. Gently heat the outside of the cake ring or tin with a blowtorch or a warm damp cloth, then slowly remove the cake.

5. Add the room temperature caramel sauce into a piping bag. Drizzle caramel sauce over the top of the mousse. Decorate with apple slices spritzed with a little lemon juice to prevent them from browning.

GINGERBREAD AND PEAR
BRANDY SNAP BASKETS

INGREDIENTS

For the brandy snaps
50g butter
50g light brown sugar
50g golden syrup
50g plain flour (gf)
½ teaspoon ground ginger

For the pears
500ml ginger beer
150g dark brown sugar
5 small pears, peeled,
   halved and cored,
   leaving stems intact

**For the gingerbread
   cream**
300ml double cream
45g light brown sugar
1 teaspoon vanilla bean
   paste
½ teaspoon ground ginger
½ teaspoon ground
   cinnamon

It's become quite a thing when gingerbread lattes come into coffee shops in the autumn. I've taken that as a cue to get baking this at home. It's a cold dessert, but still tastes comforting and warming. The gingerbread cream is a big winner and would translate so well to many different uses in warming bakes, desserts, or a luxurious hot chocolate. Brandy snaps, too, are delightful. When I bake them, I struggle to stop myself breaking off little chunks and snacking away constantly. Which is why I often end up serving only half of the baskets that I baked. Fill the brandy snaps as close to serving as possible to retain their crunch, which is vital when paired with the soft pear and cream.

METHOD

Preheat the oven to 180°C fan/ 190°C conventional/gas mark 5. Line two baking trays with non-stick baking paper. Lightly grease the outside of 4 dariole moulds or small glasses with oil or butter.

Make the brandy snaps
1. Gently heat the butter, sugar and syrup in a pan over a low heat until all melted. Remove from the heat and stir in the flour and ginger until smooth and combined. Place in the fridge – for about 30 minutes – to firm up.

2. Remove from the fridge and split into 10 even-sized portions. You can weigh these out to 20g each if you like. Roll these into small balls and place 2 to 4 balls on each prepared baking sheet spread well apart; this is important as they will spread out 2 to 3 times their unbaked size.

3. Gently press down the balls of dough a little flatter and bake for 7 to 9 minutes. The brandy snaps should be well spread, lacy and golden. Leave to cool on the tray for 2 to 3 minutes. This should allow them to firm up enough to be handled while still being warm and pliable.

4. Lift each brandy snap and place it onto the greased moulds. Use your hands to form the warm brandy snap around the mould and leave to cool on the mould for a minute until hardened. Once cool, they should slide off easily. Repeat this process for all the baked brandy snaps, then perform the baking and shaping for the next batch.

5. You must work fast to shape the brandy snaps; there is a window where they are firm enough to handle but still malleable enough to shape and manipulate. If they get too cold and brittle to shape, place them back in the oven for a minute to soften up again and repeat the shaping process.

Poach the pears
1. Bring the ginger beer and sugar up to a simmer in a large pan. Add the pear halves, ensuring they are all submerged in the liquid, so they cook evenly. Reduce the heat to a very gentle simmer and cook for 15 to 25 minutes.

Continues overleaf . . .

GINGERBREAD AND PEAR BRANDY SNAP
BASKETS CONTINUED

2. The pears are cooked once an inserted knife experiences very little resistance. At which point, remove the pears from the liquid and leave them to cool at room temperature or in the fridge.

3. Increase the heat and boil the liquid to reduce it by half into a syrup. Pour this back over the pears and set aside to cool to room temperature or in the fridge.

Make the gingerbread cream
1. Whip the double cream to medium peaks with the sugar, vanilla, ginger and cinnamon.

Assemble the baskets
1. Fill a brandy snap basket with a generous portion of the gingerbread cream – I find it easiest to pipe this in. Top with a pear half and drizzle over some of the reduced, cooled pear syrup.

2. You can serve the pears warm if you like. In which case, serve them separate from the cream, so it doesn't melt.

MARMALADE CRÈME BRÛLÉE

INGREDIENTS

100g orange marmalade
175ml milk
250ml double cream
2 oranges, zested and
   juiced
5 large egg yolks
50g caster sugar, plus extra
   for the brûlée finish
3 tablespoons Cointreau
   (or more orange juice)

Crème brûlée is a gently baked custard that should be just set and super silky and smooth. If overbaked, these can crack on top and become more solid and a little grainy to eat. If given a choice, I would prefer underbaked crème brûlée: slightly too wet but still delicious. Obviously, it's best to bake them just right, so they are soft set. The jiggle test will tell you if these are done; the edges should appear near fully set, but the centre should have a good gentle wobble. The custard can be baked well ahead of time (say, a couple of days) and placed in the fridge, so all you need to do before serving is put on the show of brûléeing the tops mere moments before everyone digs in.

I have added a bitter-sweet marmalade at the bottom of the ramekins, which works very well with the sweet cream, but this can be swapped for another preserve or removed altogether.

METHOD

Preheat the oven to 140°C fan/ 150°C conventional/gas mark 2.

1. Spread a teaspoon of marmalade over the base of 6 ramekins. Place them into a roasting tin.

2. Bring the milk and cream up to a boil in a saucepan with the orange zest. Meanwhile, gently whisk together the egg yolks, sugar, 2 tablespoons of orange juice and Cointreau.

3. Slowly pour the just-boiled milk and cream over the egg mixture, whisking as you go. Pour this mixture through a fine sieve into a jug; if there are no eggy lumps left in the sieve, you can add the zest back into the mixture.

4. Allow to settle for a couple of minutes, then use a spoon to skim off any bubbles from the surface.

5. Carefully pour the custard into the ramekins over the back of a spoon. Remove any bubbles that form on top by dabbing with a paper towel or running a blowtorch flame over the top.

6. Fill the roasting tin with recently boiled water halfway up the ramekins. Place in the oven for about 20 minutes or until the custard gently wobbles when lightly shaken. A skin may form over the top of the custard; this is absolutely fine to eat, but if you want to get rid of it, you can gently scrape it off with a teaspoon while it is warm.

7. Leave to cool until barely warm, then chill in the fridge for at least a couple of hours.

8. Sprinkle a heaped teaspoon of caster sugar over the surface of the custards and spread out into an even layer. Use a blowtorch to melt and caramelise the sugar slowly; a gentle flame for a longer time yields better results for me. Allow the caramelised sugar to cool and harden for a minute or two before serving.

CARAMEL CHOCOLATE FONDANT

INGREDIENTS

160g butter
160g dark chocolate
4 large eggs
100g caster sugar
65g plain flour (gf)
15g cocoa powder, plus
    extra for coating moulds
½ teaspoon salt
6 chocolate caramels
    (optional)
Icing sugar, for dusting

Adding chocolate caramels to the centre of these fondants is a foolproof way to create a molten-centred fondant. The caramel mixes with the fluid fondant batter, which luxuriously self-sauces the dessert on the plate. The caramel addition is not required; this fondant recipe will result in an ooey-gooey chocolatey cake without it. If overbaked or left out of the oven for too long before serving (more than 20 minutes), the fondant will dry up and not ooze in the desired way. However, the caramel centre will stay fluid and saucy even if slightly overbaked or served a little too late.

I use the sort of caramels you find in a chocolate selection box. You can also roll teaspoon-sized balls of frozen caramel sauce (page 34) and use that instead.

METHOD

Preheat the oven to 180°C fan/ 190°C conventional/gas mark 5. Grease 6 dariole moulds with a little butter. Add a heaped tablespoon of cocoa powder into the moulds and roll around to completely coat the inside. Tip out the excess powder into the next mould and repeat.

1. Gently heat the butter and chocolate in a bowl over barely simmering water or in the microwave until just melted. Leave aside to cool slightly for about 5 minutes.

2. Whisk together the eggs and sugar with an electric whisk until lightened in colour and increased in volume by just less than half (this will take 1 to 2 minutes). Sieve over the flour and cocoa powder and whisk along with the salt until smooth and combined.

3. Pour the melted butter and chocolate into the egg mixture and whisk to a smooth batter.

4. Evenly distribute the mixture between the moulds; easiest done using a piping bag. Press a chocolate caramel into the centre of each mould, if you choose. Ensure the batter covers the chocolate.

5. Bake for 12 to 15 minutes. The surface should look set, and the cakes should be pulling away slightly from the moulds. Leave to cool for about 5 minutes in the moulds before turning out, dusting with icing sugar and serving warm.

COFFEE AND CREAM ICE CREAM CAKE

INGREDIENTS

For the biscuit

100g butter, softened
60g caster sugar
1 large egg yolk
½ teaspoon salt
2 teaspoons instant coffee
    powder, dissolved in
    2 teaspoons water
160g plain flour (gf plus
    pinch of xanthan gum)
20g cocoa powder

For the ice cream filling

750ml vanilla ice cream
750ml coffee ice cream
150g walnuts, toasted and
    chopped

For the coffee cream

300ml double cream
1 teaspoon instant coffee
    powder
45g icing sugar

For the coffee ganache

75g double cream
35g dark chocolate
½ teaspoon instant coffee
    powder

I am obviously a big fan of cake, but ice cream is on another level. Cake is good, but ice cream cake, that's great! You can use homemade ice creams (see page 50), or your favourite flavours of shop-bought instead of coffee and vanilla, but the process remains the same. It's best not to use soft-serve, though. If going for flavours that might not work with the coffee chocolate biscuit, remove the coffee powder and switch the cocoa powder for more plain flour. When decorating, you have to use warm ganache – however dangerous it might feel! The ganache will freeze onto the cake very fast, so it must be warm to drip any distance down the frozen cake.

METHOD

Preheat the oven to 150°C fan/ 160°C/gas mark 3. You will need a loose-bottomed 18cm cake tin.

Make the biscuit

1. Cream the butter and sugar until light and fluffy (this will take 3 to 5 minutes).

2. Stir through the egg yolk, salt and coffee powder mixed with water. Sieve over the flour and cocoa powder and mix until it forms a stiff dough.

3. Roll out the dough between two sheets of baking paper, so it is just larger than an 18cm circle. Place this in the fridge to chill for at least 20 minutes.

4. Use the base of your 18cm cake tin as a guide to cut out a circle from the dough. Bake in the oven for 15 to 20 minutes. It's a little tricky to see when it has browned, so test if it is done by whether the biscuit's edge is firm and smells really chocolatey but not burned. The low oven temperature means it's pretty forgiving if you bake it for too long.

Assemble the cake

1. Take half of the vanilla ice cream out to thaw for about 5 minutes, so it is pliable but not liquid.

2. Place the baked biscuit into your tin and wrap the bottom of the tin in foil to prevent the ice cream from leaking. Spread the softened half of vanilla ice cream over, ensuring it is flat. Sprinkle over a layer of chopped walnuts and place back in the freezer to firm up. Take out half the coffee ice cream to thaw for about 5 minutes.

3. Spread the softened coffee ice cream over the vanilla ice cream, sprinkle over another layer of walnuts, then place back in the freezer and repeat the process with the remaining vanilla ice cream, walnuts and coffee ice cream. Reserve some walnuts for decoration, then leave to freeze completely for at least 2 hours, preferably overnight.

4. Gently warm the outside of the cake tin with a warm, damp cloth or blowtorch. Press the cake out of the tin and place it back in the freezer for at least 20 minutes.

Continues overleaf . . .

COFFEE AND CREAM ICE CREAM CAKE
CONTINUED

Make the coffee cream

1. Mix a tablespoon of cream with the coffee powder, so it dissolves. Add this to the remaining cream and icing sugar and whisk to medium peaks.

2. Take the frozen cake out of the freezer and ice it by spreading over the coffee whipped cream with a palette knife. Work fast as the cake will start to melt.

3. Press chopped walnuts into the bottom edge of the cake. Place back in the freezer to chill.

Make the coffee ganache

1. Heat the double cream until just beginning to bubble. Take off the heat and add in the chocolate and instant coffee. Gently stir until combined and smooth.

2. Pour into a piping bag, cut a small hole and pipe around the top edge of the frozen cake, stopping at intervals to create drips. From a height, drizzle a little over the top of the cake in circles.

3. Sprinkle chopped walnuts over the top edge of the cake.

ELDERFLOWER AND LEMON POSSET

INGREDIENTS

For the posset
250ml double cream
50ml elderflower cordial
50g caster sugar
2–3 lemons, zested and
    juiced (you'll need 45ml
    of juice)

For the strawberries
200g strawberries
1 tablespoon caster sugar
1 tablespoon elderflower
    cordial
2 tablespoons fresh basil
    leaves

A bit of sorcery goes on when making a posset. Warmed cream thickens with the addition of acid in the form of lemon juice which will then softly set in the fridge. It's creamy, it's sharp, it's slightly floral with elderflower: it's really good! The macerated strawberries on top are optional, but they fit so well with their self-created strawberry syrup.

You can make the possets many days ahead at a moment when you can fit in 5 minutes of hands-on cooking time. I recommend serving these alongside a round of shortbread (see page 193) to introduce a new texture.

METHOD

Make the posset
1. Place the cream, cordial, sugar and lemon zest into a pan over a medium heat. Bring to the boil, then reduce the heat and simmer for 2 minutes.

2. Remove the cream from the heat and whisk in the lemon juice gradually.

3. Strain the mixture through a sieve. Pour into small glasses or containers and place in the fridge to set for at least 4 hours or overnight.

Make the strawberries
1. Dice the strawberries and mix with the sugar and cordial, then set aside in the fridge for at least 15 minutes, so the strawberries are softened and release some juice.

2. Just before serving, finely slice the basil leaves and stir through the strawberries. Top the possets with some strawberries and their juice to serve.

CHAPTER 6
PATISSERIE

The window display of a French patisserie is something to behold. I love the characterful charm of a clearly home-baked sponge or cookie, but the striking precision of patisserie also has its place. I think the key to making good-looking and beautiful-tasting patisserie at home is to keep it simple. Some of these recipes are quite challenging as home bakes, but be assured that I don't try to replicate the most complicated techniques that often require years of professional training to achieve.

WHISKY, HONEY AND ORANGE BABAS

INGREDIENTS

For the savarin dough
100g whole milk
7g fast action yeast
40g caster sugar
270g strong bread flour
7g salt
4 large eggs
95g unsalted butter, very soft

For a GF savarin dough
100g whole milk
7g fast action yeast
40g caster sugar
270g gluten-free plain flour
1½ teaspoons xanthan gum
10g psyllium husk powder
7g salt
½ teaspoon cider vinegar
4 large eggs
95g unsalted butter, very soft

For the crème légère
1 large egg yolk
15g caster sugar
10g cornflour
85g whole milk
2 tablespoons Cointreau
    (or orange juice)
100ml double cream
10g icing sugar
50g marmalade

For the syrup
2 large oranges, juiced and
    peeled
150ml whisky
    (or more orange juice)
225ml water, plus an
    additional 100ml
175g honey
150g caster sugar, plus an
    additional 50g

I love whisky, but my knowledge is limited, so I tested this recipe on a friend who is in the whisky industry and asked for some advice on the whiskies that could be used. These style recommendations would be great in this sweet bake:

- Speyside single malt Scotch (my favourite) and triple distilled Irish whiskeys are typically light, fruity and sweet. This is the best choice if you prefer a subtle flavour that won't overpower the bake.

- Whiskies matured in American casks and American bourbon can deliver a cakey-sweet profile with vanilla and coconut notes.

- European ex-sherry casks can offer Christmas spice flavours which will play well with the orange in the babas.

Babas are made with an enriched, yeasted dough which is trickier to bake gluten-free. I have added specific notes on how to best bake this gluten-free.

METHOD

Preheat the oven to 180°C fan/ 190°C conventional/gas mark 5. You will need an 8-hole, 5cm silicone cube mould, or can instead grease a 12-hole muffin tin with butter.

Make the savarin dough
1. Gently warm the milk to body temperature. In a bowl, mix the yeast, warm milk and sugar. Set aside for about 5 minutes until slightly frothy.

- Standard – In the bowl of a stand mixer, place the flour and salt, mix with a paddle attachment and add the milk mixture. Add the eggs and mix at medium speed for about 3 minutes. Add the butter about a tablespoon at a time until all added. Crank up the speed and mix on medium-high for 5 to 8 minutes. It should be super shiny and stretchy, almost a cross between a dough and a batter.

- Gluten-free – In the bowl of a stand mixer, place the flour, xanthan gum, psyllium husk powder and salt, mix with a paddle attachment then add the milk mixture and cider vinegar. Add the eggs and mix at medium speed. Add the butter about a tablespoon at a time until all added. Crank up the speed and mix on medium-high for about 5 minutes. It should look like a very thick, almost gloopy batter.

2. Fill a piping bag with the dough. Next, fill each of your moulds (you will get 8 to 12 babas) about half full by piping out the dough and cutting it off with scissors (cutting with scissors is not necessary for GF dough). Cover with cling film sprinkled with a little oil and leave to prove for 60 to 90 minutes in a warm place. The dough should at least double in size and be peeking over the top of the moulds.

Continues overleaf . . .

3. Bake the babas in the oven for 15 to 20 minutes or until deeply golden on top. Leave to cool in the mould.

4. Once cooled, remove the babas from the moulds and slice the domed tops off them to create uniform cubes.

Make the crème légère

1. Whisk the egg yolk with the sugar until combined. Stir through the cornflour, so it is incorporated. Whisk in the milk and Cointreau (or orange juice substitute).

2. Pour this mixture into a non-stick pan and place over a high heat, constantly stirring until it bubbles and thickens. This is a crème pat. Remove from the heat, cover the surface with cling film or baking paper and leave to cool to room temperature.

3. Once the crème pat is cool, whisk the cream with the icing sugar to medium-firm peaks. Beat the cooled crème pat to smooth it out, then fold through the whipped cream until fully combined. Place in a piping bag in the fridge until ready to be used.

4. Sieve the marmalade and fill a piping bag with it.

Make the syrup

1. Use a vegetable peeler to peel the oranges. Cut these strips into thin slices.

2. Add the orange juice and peel, whisky, water, honey and sugar into a saucepan (excluding the additional sugar and water), and bring to a boil stirring occasionally.

3. Once the mixture has boiled and the sugar has dissolved, remove it from the heat.

4. Dunk the babas into the warm syrup and hold them there for about 3 to 4 minutes, flipping upside down halfway through. For the last couple, the syrup level may be quite low. For these, rotate the babas more frequently to ensure all sides are soaked.

5. Remove from the syrup and place on a wire rack for excess syrup to drain away.

6. Now place the syrup and orange peel back on a medium-low heat with the additional water and sugar. Simmer for about 15 minutes until the syrup has reduced, and the orange zest looks slightly translucent. Drain the orange zest and set it aside for decoration.

Assemble the babas

1. Pipe a small portion of crème légère into the centre of the babas, entering via the cut side of the sponge. Follow this by piping a dod of marmalade into the crème.

2. Clean the piping bags and pipe crème légère onto the top of the babas. I like to pipe a large blob onto half the babas then cut an angled hole into the bag and pipe swooshy lines onto the other babas. Next pipe over with tiny dots of marmalade. Top with the candied orange peel.

CHOCOLATE ORANGE MACARONS

INGREDIENTS

For the macarons
110g ground almonds
110g icing sugar
2 large egg whites
Orange gel food colouring
110g caster sugar
2 tablespoons water

For the ganache
75g double cream
75g milk chocolate

For the filling
150g marmalade

Macarons are a little tricky to bake. The key to their success is in the stage called the macaronage. This is when you are folding the meringue through the almond mixture. If you fold for too long at this stage, the batter will be too runny, and the macarons won't hold their shape when piped. If you mix too little at this stage, the tops of the macarons will never sit flat or be smooth. I would encourage you to err on the side of undermixing if you are making macarons for the first time and then adjust by mixing for a couple more folds the next time you bake. Practice will help you feel out the correct consistency.

METHOD

Preheat the oven to 140°C fan/ 150°C conventional/gas mark 2. Line 2 baking trays with non-stick baking paper.

Make the macarons

1. Add the ground almonds and icing sugar in a bowl along with 1 egg white. Mix into a thick paste and add gel food colouring to create a bright orange colour.

2. Add the sugar into a pan (not non-stick) with the water and stir over a high heat until the sugar has dissolved and the mixture begins to bubble. Once bubbling, stop stirring but leave the syrup on a high heat.

3. Meanwhile, add the remaining egg white into a bowl and whisk with an electric hand whisk until frothy.

4. Take the temperature of the sugar. When it reaches 118–121°C, take it off the heat and slowly pour it into the egg white while whisking at high speed. Continue until the meringue has cooled to room temperature and is thick and glossy.

5. Add a third of the meringue into the bowl with the ground almond mixture and fold again until fully combined. Add in the remaining meringue and fold again until thoroughly combined. At this point the batter will slowly run off the spatula in thick ribbons, sinking back into the mixture about 15 seconds after leaving a trail. If the batter is too thick, keep folding until you reach the thick ribbon texture. Add the batter to a piping bag fitted with a 1cm nozzle.

6. Pipe small rounds, about 3cm in diameter, of the macaron batter onto the prepared baking trays. Try to make them all the same size so the finished macarons will match and fit. To make this easier you can use a pencil to draw guide outlines around a cookie cutter on the underside of the baking paper.

7. Bang the trays firmly on your work surface a couple of times to knock out air bubbles from the batter. Use a toothpick to pop any large air bubbles on the surface of the macarons.

Continues overleaf . . .

8. Leave the trays to sit uncovered at room temperature for about 30 minutes. After this time, they should form a skin and not feel wet to a gentle touch. If they still feel sticky, leave them to dry for longer.

9. Bake for 15 to 17 minutes. They should feel crisp to a gentle touch, and the edges of each macaron should appear almost to be pulling away from the paper it sits on. Leave the macarons to cool to room temperature on the paper before carefully peeling them off. If they stay stuck once cool, they were underbaked.

Make the ganache

1. Heat the cream in a pan until it just begins to bubble. Remove from the heat, add the chocolate and stir gently until combined and smooth.

2. Chill in the fridge or at a cold room temperature until the mixture has thickened to a soft, spreadable consistency that holds its shape. If it becomes too firm, leave it out at a warm room temperature or blast in the microwave in 2 second increments until easily spreadable.

3. Fill a piping bag with the ganache. Cut a ¾ cm hole in the bag.

Assemble the macarons

1. Pair up the macarons with other similar sized and shaped macarons.

2. Pipe a ring of ganache around the perimeter of the flat side of half the macarons, leaving a hole in the centre.

3. Fill a piping bag with the marmalade. Cut a hole in the piping bag and fill the centre of the ganache with the marmalade

4. Top each filled macaron half with its partner. Leave the macarons aside for a couple of hours or in the fridge overnight before serving.

PISTACHIO RELIGIEUSE

INGREDIENTS

1 quantity choux pastry and craquelin (page 17) (gf)

For the crème légère
100g pistachio paste (available online)
200ml whole milk
2 large egg yolks
50g caster sugar
10g cornflour
½ teaspoon salt
1 teaspoon vanilla bean paste
150ml double cream
15g icing sugar

To assemble
150g raspberry jam
20g pistachios, halved

These two choux buns stacked atop one another gain their name from their resemblance to a nun wearing a habit. Honestly, I don't see it, but what I do see is a beautiful little pastry that I like the look of so much it has been my phone wallpaper for an entire year. These are filled with a decadent crème légère flavoured with the 'king of the nuts', pistachio. You can, optionally, pipe a dod of raspberry jam into the choux buns to bring zip and sweetness to the otherwise creamy, rich filling.

METHOD

Preheat the oven to 175°C fan/ 185°C conventional/gas mark 4.5. Line two baking trays with non-stick baking paper.

Bake the choux

1. Make the choux dough and craquelin as outlined on page 17. Pipe 2cm and 4cm diameter circles of choux onto the lined baking trays. You should get about 20 of each size. You will likely need to pipe at least 2 batches to ensure you leave plenty of space between the choux. Top each bun with a disc of craquelin the same size as the bun.

2. Place the trays in the oven to bake. The small buns should bake in about 20 to 25 minutes; the large in 30 to 35 minutes. Remove the small buns once they are deep golden brown, crisp and hollow, and place the larger buns back in until they are baked too.

3. Use a piping nozzle to poke a hole into the bottom of each choux bun before setting aside to cool.

Make the crème légère

1. Mix the pistachio paste with the milk and place over a low heat in a pan, so it slowly comes up to a simmer.

2. Meanwhile, whisk the egg yolks with the sugar, then whisk through the cornflour, salt and vanilla. Once the milk begins to simmer, gradually pour it into the egg mixture while whisking. Pour this back into the pan and cook over a high heat, constantly stirring, until it bubbles and thickens. This is a crème pat. Pour into a clean bowl, cover the surface with cling film or baking paper and leave to cool to room temperature.

3. Whip the cream with the icing sugar to medium peaks. Beat the cooled crème pat to smooth it out, then fold through the whipped cream until fully combined, making your crème légère.

Assemble the religieuse

1. Fill a piping bag with this mixture. Pipe it into all the buns, so they are about four fifths full. Fill another bag with the jam and pipe into the filled buns until the filling just begins to overflow. You should have some pistachio cream left over.

2. Stack one small bun onto a large bun using a little pistachio cream. Pipe a tiny dod of the pistachio cream onto the top choux bun and top with a pistachio half. Pipe tiny dots of pistachio cream around the join of the two buns as a collar.

MONT BLANCS

INGREDIENTS

For the meringue
3 large egg whites
150g caster sugar
50g icing sugar

For the filling
250g sweetened chestnut
  purée
75g hazelnuts, roasted and
  roughly chopped

For the Chantilly cream
300ml double cream
30g icing sugar
1 tablespoon vanilla bean
  paste

Mont Blanc is a classic little French pastry made with chestnut, cream and meringue, sponge or biscuit and designed to resemble its mountainous namesake. The dessert is typically topped with intricately piped chestnut cream and dusted with icing sugar to give the mountain-like appearance. I have changed the design of these Mont Blancs while keeping in mind the inspiration of the bake, partly for the fun of creating a new design and also because the technique for the classic design is rather fiddly and difficult to achieve!

METHOD

Preheat the oven to 110°C fan/ 120°C conventional/gas mark ½. Place an upturned silicone hemisphere mould on a baking tray. This recipe makes 6 x 6cm hemispheres.

Make the meringue

1. Whisk the egg whites with a stand mixer or electric hand whisk until they have a cloud-like texture.

2. Gradually add in the caster sugar about a tablespoon at a time, whisking at medium speed. Wait about 15 seconds between each addition of sugar to make sure it dissolves properly into the meringue.

3. Once you have added all the caster sugar, briefly whisk through the icing sugar until combined.

4. Fill a piping bag fitted with a large round nozzle with the meringue.

5. Pipe the meringue over the curved outside of your 6 silicone moulds, holding the piping bag vertically and piping from the top of the mould. The meringue should move down the sides of the moulds. This will create a bowl-like meringue once baked. Flatten the top of the meringues with a knife so that they will sit flat when they are upturned.

6. Place the meringue in the oven for 60 to 90 minutes. The tops of the meringue should feel firm, and you should be able to carefully lift the meringue off the mould without it breaking.

7. Once baked, lift the meringues off the mould and invert to leave to cool on the flat firm side of the meringue.

Fill the meringues

1. Once the meringues are cool, place them on your serving plates. Fill the hole of the meringue with the chestnut purée and top with chopped hazelnuts. Reserve some hazelnuts for later.

Make the Chantilly cream

1. Whip the cream with the icing sugar and vanilla to medium peaks. Fill a piping bag fitted with a large round nozzle with the cream.

2. Pipe the cream vertically onto the chestnut purée, pulling the bag up gradually as you pipe the cream to create a large peak.

3. Top the cream with pieces of roasted hazelnuts to decorate.

CARAMELISED WHITE CHOCOLATE MADELEINES

INGREDIENTS

120g butter, plus extra for
    greasing
2 large eggs
80g caster sugar
20g clear honey
120g self-raising flour (gf)
½ teaspoon salt
200g caramelised white
    chocolate (page 31)

*My mum described this recipe as a 'hug in cake form' – a lovely compliment
for a madeleine, which is such a simple and comforting little cake. In making
this batter, the butter is browned, which adds more interest and layers to the
flavours and ties in with the caramelised white chocolate that proudly coats and
highlights the distinctive shell texture of the sponges.*

METHOD

Preheat the oven to 180°C fan/
190°C conventional/gas mark 5. You
will need a 12-hole madeleine tin,
greased with butter if not non-stick.

1. Add the butter to a heavy-based
   pan over a high heat, stirring
   occasionally. Once the bubbles
   subside and the butter smells nutty
   and turns a brown colour, pour it
   into a heatproof bowl and leave
   to cool until just warm.

2. Whisk the eggs with the sugar
   and honey until combined. Sieve
   over the flour and whisk this into
   the egg mix along with the salt.

3. Pour in the warm, not hot, brown
   butter and whisk to a smooth
   batter. Pour the batter into a
   piping bag and leave to chill in
   the fridge for at least an hour.

4. Pipe the chilled batter into a
   madeleine tin, filling each hole
   about three quarters full. Bake in
   the oven for about 10 minutes, or
   until a deep, even golden colour.

5. Leave the madeleines to cool in the
   tin before removing. Clean the tin.

6. Melt the caramelised white
   chocolate. Pipe a generous
   portion of the melted chocolate
   into each hole of the tin. The
   chocolate should cover about a
   quarter to a third of the mould.
   Press a cooled madeleine into
   the melted chocolate in the tin,
   pressing until you can barely see
   the chocolate peeking out the
   sides. Place these in the freezer for
   at least 30 minutes.

7. Push one end of the frozen
   madeleines to dislodge the
   chocolate and remove them from
   the tin. Allow them to come back
   to room temperature, chocolate
   facing up, before serving.

ROSE AND RASPBERRY FRIANDS

INGREDIENTS

75g butter, plus extra for greasing
1 large egg white
90g icing sugar
25g plain flour (gf + pinch xanthan gum)
50g ground almonds
25g pistachios, chopped
1 teaspoon rosewater
50g fresh raspberries, halved
Icing sugar, to dust

My flatmates have been incredibly supportive during the process of writing this book and have offered feedback on recipe tests along the way, typically with quite positive opinions and the occasional piece of helpful criticism. However, when it came to this recipe, my flatmate, Fraser, provided the wonderfully constructive feedback of 'That was gross!' The lesson is that if you don't like rosewater, you shouldn't bake this. If you do like rosewater, then I recommend you give it a go!

METHOD

Preheat the oven to 200°C fan/ 210°C conventional/gas mark 7. You will need a 16-hole mini oval silicone mould or mini muffin tin, greased with butter if the tin is not non-stick.

1. Melt the butter and set it aside to cool for about 5 minutes.

2. Lightly whisk the egg white for about 20 seconds until frothy but without structure. Add in the icing sugar, flour and ground almonds and stir together until combined.

3. Add in the cooled melted butter along with the chopped pistachios and rosewater, and stir until fully combined. Fill a piping bag with the mixture.

4. Pipe the mixture into the friand moulds to just below the top. Top each portion with a half raspberry. Bake for about 10 minutes or until golden on top. Leave to cool for about 5 minutes before turning out to cool completely.

5. Lightly dust with icing sugar before serving.

BLACK FOREST GATEAU

INGREDIENTS

For the sponge
75g plain flour (gf)
30g cocoa powder
½ teaspoon baking powder (gf)
½ teaspoon bicarbonate of soda
115g caster sugar
½ teaspoon salt
1 large egg
85ml milk
40ml olive oil
1 teaspoon vanilla extract
50ml boiling water
150g Amarena cherries, drained (reserve the syrup)

For the mousse
150ml whole milk
2 large egg yolks
35g caster sugar
150g dark chocolate
150g double cream

For the set cream
2 sheets leaf gelatine (any grade)
5 tablespoons Amarena cherry syrup
230ml double cream
25g icing sugar
1 teaspoon vanilla bean paste

For the mirror glaze
90g water
75g caster sugar
105g glucose syrup
10g cocoa powder
3 sheets leaf gelatine (any grade)
60g condensed milk
90g dark chocolate

At least a dozen friends have tested this bake, and all gave that kind of feedback where you can tell you got something right putting the recipe together. The cherries are a large part of this dessert tasting so good. I buy Amarena Fabbri cherries in syrup online. Laura, my *Bake Off* friend, introduced me to them, and I will be forever grateful for this. They taste incredible and are well worth the price tag! You might like fresh cherries, too, to decorate the gateau.

METHOD

Preheat the oven to 170°C fan/ 180°C conventional/gas mark 4. Grease and base line a 20cm square tin.

Bake the sponge
1. Sieve the flour, cocoa powder, baking powder and bicarbonate of soda into a large bowl and mix with the sugar and salt.

2. Whisk in the egg, milk, oil and vanilla until smooth and shiny.

3. Gradually whisk in the water to reach a smooth, very thin batter.

4. Pour into the prepared tin and bake for about 20 minutes, or until a skewer comes out clean and you can hear a gentle bubble. Leave to cool in or out of the tin.

5. Trim the top off the cake, leaving it about 1–1.5cm tall. Place the cake on a baking sheet and cut it out using a 16–18cm, 4cm tall square cake frame. Alternatively, cut to a 16–18cm square and place in a loose-bottomed cake tin.

6. Pour 3 to 4 tablespoons of the reserved Amarena cherry juice over the cake and lay the drained cherries over the base sponge evenly dispersed, leaving a border between them and the cake frame or tin.

Make the mousse
1. Heat the milk in a pan until just boiling. Whisk together the egg yolks and sugar in a bowl. Pour the hot milk over the yolk mix, whisking constantly. Return this to the pan and cook over a low heat until it is thickened and reaches 75–82°C.

2. Take the custard off the heat and stir in the chocolate until smooth. Leave this to cool at room temperature.

3. Once the chocolate custard has reached about 35°C, whip the cream to medium-firm peaks. Fold the whipped cream through the chocolate custard until smooth and one consistent colour.

4. Pour the mousse into the cake frame over the sponge and cherries. Tap the tray, so the mousse levels off. Place this in the freezer to firm up.

Make the set cream
1. Soak the gelatine sheets in cold water for a couple of minutes.

2. Heat the cherry syrup until barely steaming. Squeeze out the excess liquid from the gelatine, then stir the gelatine into the warm cherry juice off the heat, so it melts. Set aside to cool at room temperature until no longer warm to the touch.

Continues overleaf . . .

BLACK FOREST GATEAU
CONTINUED

3. Whisk the cream with the icing sugar and vanilla to medium peaks. Add in the gelatine-cherry mixture and briefly whisk through until combined.

4. Add the cream into the mould over the chocolate mousse. Make sure you fill all of the gaps. Level off the top with a palette knife; this is very easy if using a cake frame, as you can simply scrape across the top of the frame with a large palette knife.

5. Place in the freezer for a couple of hours, so it is completely frozen.

Make the mirror glaze

1. Put the water, sugar, glucose syrup and cocoa powder in a pan over high heat. Bring to the boil while whisking. Soak the gelatine in cold water for a couple of minutes.

2. Remove the pan from the heat, stir in the condensed milk, squeeze out excess liquid from the gelatine, and stir the gelatine into the mix.

3. Pour this mixture over the chocolate in a bowl and stir until melted and combined.

4. Pass through a sieve and leave to cool out at room temperature, stirring occasionally.

Assemble your gateau

1. Remove the gateau from the freezer. Gently warm the cake frame or tin with a blowtorch and remove. Place the cake back in the freezer, so the outside is completely frozen.

2. Place the frozen cake onto a wire cooling rack over a rimmed baking tray. Once the mirror glaze has cooled to between 30–40°C (or about body temperature to the touch), pour it over the frozen cake from a jug. Start by pouring it over the edges of the cake to ensure all the sides are covered, then pour the rest into the centre. Tap the cooling rack to encourage excess glaze to drip down the sides of the cake and create a level top.

3. You can keep any excess glaze in a sealed container in the fridge for a couple of weeks and use it again by gently melting and using when the glaze is 30–40°C.

4. Transfer the frozen gateau to your serving plate using a cake lifter while touching as little of the mirror glaze as possible. Place back in the fridge until ready to serve. At which point you can decorate it with fresh cherries.

COCONUT AND LIME PARIS-BREST

INGREDIENTS

For the pastry
1 quantity choux pastry
   (page 17) (gf)
75g desiccated coconut

For the crème légère
300ml coconut milk
3 large egg yolks
75g caster sugar
30g cornflour
2 teaspoons vanilla bean
   paste
225ml double cream
25g icing sugar

To assemble
1 quantity lime juice curd
   (page 41)
1 lime, zested, to decorate

The Paris-Brest is a circular choux pastry dessert designed to resemble a bike wheel commemorating the Paris-Brest-Paris bike race. It is classically filled with a praline cream, but this version is a little zestier with coconut and lime. I don't often pipe into templates, but it is necessary to create a good shape for these.

METHOD

Preheat the oven to 175°C fan/ 185°C conventional/gas mark 4.5. Line 2 baking trays with non-stick baking paper. Dip an 8cm cutter in cornflour, then pat this on the baking paper to create 8 to 10 outlines.

Make the choux pastry rings

1. Make the choux pastry as instructed on page 17, and fill a piping bag fitted with a large star nozzle with many teeth.

2. Pipe the dough onto the baking paper in rings inside your cornflour outlines. Release the pressure as you reach the join and drag the straggling pastry around the ring, leaving a slight overlap.

3. Sprinkle the desiccated coconut all over the choux rings, completely covering the choux.

4. Bake for about 30 to 35 minutes until the buns are well risen, golden and crisp. If the coconut starts to turns too dark, turn the oven down to 140°C fan/150°C conventional/gas mark 2 after 20 to 25 minutes and bake for a further 15 to 20 minutes, so the choux continues to bake without burning.

Make the crème légère
1. Heat the coconut milk in a pan until it begins to bubble.

2. Meanwhile, whisk the egg yolks with the caster sugar, then whisk through the cornflour and vanilla. Once the milk has just started to bubble, slowly pour it into the egg mixture while whisking.

3. Return this to the pan over a high heat, constantly stirring until the mixture bubbles and thickens. This is a crème pat. Remove from the heat, cover the surface with cling film or baking paper and cool to room temperature.

4. Whisk the cream with the icing sugar to medium peaks. Beat the cooled crème pat to loosen it up, then fold through the whipped cream until fully combined.

5. Fill a piping bag fitted with a large open star nozzle with the crème légère and chill until ready to use.

Assemble the Paris-Brest
1. Slice the choux rings in half horizontally. Fill a piping bag with the lime curd and pipe this into the bottom half of the choux ring.

2. Pipe the coconut crème légère into the bottom half of the choux. Hold the piping bag vertically and pipe large tall dots of the cream.

3. Dust half of the top ring with icing sugar, then top the filled bottom halves with the tops. Zest over some lime.

VANILLA AND PECAN GATEAU ST HONORÉ

INGREDIENTS

For the pastry
½ quantity rough puff pastry
(page 14) (gf)
20g icing sugar

For the choux
½ quantity choux pastry and
craquelin (page 17) (gf)

For the pecan praline
75g pecans
50g sugar
1 tablespoon water
¼ teaspoon salt

For the crème patisserie
400ml whole milk
4 large egg yolks
100g light brown sugar
30g cornflour
2 teaspoons vanilla bean
paste

For the Chantilly cream
300ml double cream
30g icing sugar
1 tablespoon vanilla bean
paste

Rough puff pastry, choux, praline, crème pat, Chantilly and piping skills are all on show in my version of this classic. However, every step is distinct, simple, and not overly time-dependent, so you can easily break down the stages in this bake, making it far more manageable. And at the end of a big baking session, you'll have a dessert fit for the patron saint of bakers.

METHOD

Preheat the oven to 190°C fan/ 200°C conventional/gas mark 6. Line a baking tray with non-stick baking paper.

Bake the rough puff pastry
1. Make your pastry, then roll it out on a lightly floured surface until ¾ cm thick. Cut out a 23cm circle from it, using a cake tin as a guide. Place onto your baking tray.

2. Dust the pastry by sieving over icing sugar to cover it completely. Cover with a further sheet of baking paper and top with another tray to weigh it down.

3. Bake the pastry covered for 20 minutes, then uncover and bake for a further 5 to 10 minutes or until deeply golden. Leave to cool.

Reduce the oven to 175°C fan/ 185°C conventional/gas mark 4.5.

Bake the choux
1. Make the choux dough as instructed on page 17. Pipe 2cm circles of the dough onto lined baking trays, top with craquelin and bake for 30 to 35 minutes or until deeply golden and very crisp.

2. Slice the top quarter off each bun and leave aside to cool.

Make the pecan praline
1. Make a praline with the pecans as instructed on page 35. Once coated in caramel, separate the pecans as best as you can so they cool individually.

2. Roughly chop two thirds of the praline you have created, keeping some whole pecans for later.

Make the crème pâtissèrie
1. Use the ingredients listed and follow the method on page 46. Cover with cling film or baking paper and cool in the fridge.

Assemble the gateau
1. Beat the crème pat to smooth it out then fill a piping bag with it. Use about half to pipe a layer onto the centre of your pastry disc, leaving a 1cm gap to the perimeter edge. Sprinkle a layer of chopped praline over the crème pat, reserving some for later.

2. Fill the bases of the choux buns with the remaining crème pat, filling them proud above the rim, then top with the sliced-off lids.

3. Place 8 filled choux buns onto the puff pastry around the perimeter, evenly spacing them.

4. Make Chantilly cream (page 43), and fill a piping bag with it. Cut a 1cm wide hole into it at a 45 degree angle. Pipe short straight lines in between the buns with the short cut side of the bag facing up. Pipe into the centre of the gateau with long curved motions.

5. Place a choux bun in the centre of the gateau. Top the gateau with chopped praline, then top the cream between the buns with whole praline pecans.

Peter, aged 3

CHAPTER 7
LITTLE BAKES
FOR KIDS AND BEGINNERS

I have loved baking since I was five or six, creating bakes similar to those in this chapter. As I've grown, practice means that I now make some more complicated bakes, but I've never stopped taking pleasure from these treats. If you're new to baking, all you need to focus on is having fun in the kitchen, making a mess if you choose and then digging into the tasty treats you create.

MINI CARROT CAKES

Carrot cake keeps beautifully moist for a good amount of time. Oil-based cakes like this hold onto moisture better than butter-based ones, plus the grated carrots contain a lot of moisture and help make the cake so soft and delicious. The batter will be wet before baking, so I find the cleanest way to fill the moulds is by pouring it in from a large jug. But it doesn't really matter if you make a mess, that's a big part of the fun of baking!

The key to making the frosting is not to mix too much when you add the cream cheese. This will slacken the mixture and make it runny. Instead, beat the butter and sugar together for a good few minutes, then gently mix through the cream cheese until just combined.

INGREDIENTS

For the cakes
100g light brown sugar
100g oil
2 large eggs
140g carrots, coarsely grated (about 2–3 carrots)
100g walnuts, chopped
1 teaspoon vanilla extract
100g self-raising flour (gf)
1 teaspoon bicarbonate of soda
1 teaspoon ground cinnamon
½ teaspoon ground mixed spice
½ teaspoon salt

For the frosting
100g butter
150g icing sugar
150g cream cheese
20g walnuts, to decorate

METHOD

Preheat the oven to 170°C fan/180°C conventional/ gas mark 4. Use a mini cake mould or fill a 12-hole muffin tin with cupcake cases.

MAKE THE CAKES

1. Whisk together the sugar, oil and eggs in a large mixing bowl. Add in the carrots, walnuts and vanilla. Then sieve over the flour, bicarbonate of soda, cinnamon, mixed spice and salt. Fold this all through until combined.

2. Fill the cake moulds or muffin cases about two thirds full. Bake for 15 minutes or until a skewer comes away clean. Leave to cool.

MAKE THE FROSTING

1. Beat the butter until smooth and light. Add the icing sugar in 3 batches, beating for 2 minutes after each addition. Add the cream cheese in three 50g portions, mixing through until just combined after each addition.

2. Pipe or spread the frosting over the cooled cakes and top with a walnut half.

SCONES

Scones are a brilliant first bake. They are wonderfully simple, take very little time to prepare and don't create much washing-up. Scones are also a fantastic blank canvas to get creative with toppings. Eat them with classic clotted cream and jam, Chantilly cream and a jazzy curd, or anything else you think sounds exciting! You can also omit the sugar and make savoury scones to eat with soup; this is my mum's favourite lunch.

This recipe has the option to make white chocolate and cranberry scones, a delicious combination, but you can switch out these add-ins for any of your favourites.

INGREDIENTS

Makes 6 scones.

200g self-raising flour
   (gf + ½ teaspoon xanthan gum)
2 tablespoons caster sugar
1 teaspoon baking powder (gf)
½ teaspoon salt
35g butter
80ml milk
1 large egg
75g white chocolate chips (optional)
50g dried cranberries (optional)
1 additional egg, for egg wash
2 tablespoons demerara sugar (optional)

METHOD

Preheat the oven to 200°C fan/210°C conventional/gas mark 7. Line a baking tray with baking paper.

1. Mix the flour, sugar, baking powder, salt and xanthan gum (if gf) in a mixing bowl. Rub the butter in using your fingertips until the mixture resembles fine breadcrumbs.

2. Briefly whisk the milk through the egg. Add this to the dry ingredients with the white chocolate and cranberries, if desired, and mix in with a table knife. Get your hands in and gently work it together into a soft ball of dough. A softer dough will get a better rise.

3. Generously flour your work surface and turn the dough out onto it. Use a rolling pin or your palms to flatten the dough out to a height of between 3 and 3.5cm. Use a 6cm round cutter to cut out the scones. Transfer them to your baking tray.

4. Brush the tops of the scones with egg wash and optionally sprinkle the demerara sugar over for a crunchy sweet top. Bake for 10 to 12 minutes or until well risen and golden.

SHORTBREAD

A good Scottish shortbread should taste wonderfully buttery and have a light, crumbly texture. Shortbread gets its name from the crumbly texture, which is called 'short'. The term 'short' relates to the length of gluten strands that form in the biscuit dough. A loaf of bread has 'long' developed strands of gluten that make the dough stretchy. The high-fat content of shortbread prevents long gluten strands and gives the biscuits their delightful texture.

If you make this with regular flour, be careful not to handle or knead the dough too much as this can encourage long gluten formations, which will make the shortbread tough. This area of baking is almost easier to bake gluten-free: you can't overwork the gluten as none is present!

INGREDIENTS

Makes about 18 biscuits.

100g unsalted butter, softened
25g caster sugar
25g icing sugar
½ teaspoon salt
125g plain flour (gf + ¼ teaspoon xanthan gum)
25g cornflour
30g demerara sugar (optional)

METHOD

Preheat the oven to 150°C fan/160°C conventional/ gas mark 3. Line 1 or 2 baking trays with baking paper.

1. Cream the butter with the caster sugar, icing sugar and salt using an electric whisk or stand mixer until light and fluffy (this takes 3 to 5 minutes).

2. Stir through the remaining ingredients, excluding the demerara sugar, and gently work it together with your hands until it comes together into a dough.

3. Roll the dough into a rough log about 18cm long. If you want to add a sugary crunch around the biscuits' edge, roll it in the demerara sugar.

4. Wrap the dough in baking paper or cling film. Twist the ends of the paper or film and roll again, so it is tight around the dough. Place in the fridge to chill for at least 20 minutes.

5. Take the dough out of the fridge and slice into discs about ¾ cm thick.

6. Place the biscuits onto your baking trays and bake in the oven for about 15 minutes or until lightly golden. The biscuits will be very soft out of the oven but will be firm enough to handle once cool.

MILLIONAIRE'S SHORTBREAD DOMES

Chocolate, caramel and shortbread, that's a winning combo! These little domes are a fancy way to serve the classic traybake that's everyone's favourite. The domes are very small and dainty, so they can be a little fiddly to put together. However, if any turn out more broken or messier than you would like, you can enjoy a chef's perk and hide the evidence with a tasty post-baking snack!

INGREDIENTS

Makes 30 to 40 domes.

For the shortbread
50g unsalted butter, softened
30g caster sugar
1 large egg yolk
½ teaspoon salt
90g plain flour (gf plus pinch xanthan gum)

For the filling
250g dark chocolate
1 quantity salted caramel sauce (high butter,
    low cream), or 1 tin of caramel

METHOD

Preheat the oven to 150°C fan/160°C conventional/ gas mark 3. Line a baking tray with baking paper. You will need a small hemisphere or cake pop mould.

MAKE THE SHORTBREAD

1. Cream the butter and sugar until light and fluffy (this will take 3 to 5 minutes).

2. Stir through the remaining ingredients until it forms a stiff dough. Gently work together into a ball using your hands.

3. Roll out the dough between two sheets of baking paper until about ¼ cm thick. Place this in the fridge to chill for at least 20 minutes.

4. Find a cutter that is just smaller than the opening to your hemisphere or cake pop mould. Cut discs of the shortbread using this cutter, transfer to your baking tray and bake for 10 to 12 minutes or until lightly golden around the edges.

FILL AND ASSEMBLE

1. Melt 150g of the chocolate, remove from the heat, then stir through a further 50g until all melted. Pour a teaspoon of chocolate into each mould and use the back of a teaspoon to spread it around the inside of the mould, completely covering it. Leave this to set at room temperature.

2. Spoon or pipe the cooled caramel into the set chocolate domes filling them about five sixths full. Place a shortbread round into each dome. Melt the remaining 50g of chocolate and fill a piping bag with it. Cut a very fine hole from the piping bag and fill any gaps between the shortbread and moulds or caramel with chocolate. Leave this to chill in the fridge for at least 30 minutes.

3. Once chilled, pop out from the moulds and dig in!

RASPBERRY EMPIRE BISCUITS

Empire biscuits were my favourite after-school treat from the local bakers on a Friday. Two slightly yielding and satisfyingly soft shortbread biscuits filled with a dod of jam is a good thing. I'm not looking for a super crunchy or snappy biscuit here; I want a slight bend and softness. To get that, make sure not to roll the dough too thin or bake it for too long.

INGREDIENTS

Makes about 16 empire biscuits.

For the biscuits
200g unsalted butter, softened
125g caster sugar
1 large egg
1 teaspoon vanilla extract
½ teaspoon salt
350g plain flour (gf + ½ teaspoon xanthan gum)

For the icing
150g icing sugar
2–3 tablespoons raspberry cordial
  (or substitute for water)

For the filling
150g raspberry jam
  (see page 43 if you'd like to make your own)

To decorate
Fresh raspberries

METHOD

Preheat the oven to 160°C fan/170°C conventional/gas mark 3.5.

MAKE THE BISCUITS

1. Cream the butter and sugar until light and fluffy (this takes about 3 to 5 minutes).

2. Stir through the remaining ingredients until it forms a stiff dough. Gently work together into a ball with your hands.

3. Roll out the dough between 2 sheets of baking paper until about ½ cm thick. Place this in the fridge to chill for at least 20 minutes.

4. Cut circles from the dough (I tend to cut 7cm), place onto baking trays and bake for 10 to 12 minutes or until lightly browning around the edges.

5. Mix the icing sugar with the cordial, so it becomes a thick yet fluid consistency. Gradually add the liquid to make sure it doesn't become too thin.

ASSEMBLE

1. Take half of the biscuits, dip the top of them into the icing, lift out and shake off as much of the excess as possible. Run your finger around the edge of the biscuits to make a clean edge. Place half a raspberry on the centre of the biscuit.

2. Take an uniced biscuit, flip it upside down. Dod a teaspoon of jam onto the biscuit's flat side and spread it out not quite to the edge of the biscuit. Sandwich the biscuits together by placing an iced biscuit on top.

MUM'S CORONATION SLICE

I have to credit my mum and gran for this recipe. My gran initially adapted it from the *High Kirk Cookbook* and would bake it as a teatime treat for my mum when she was little. My mum then took on the recipe and found great success baking coronation slice for church coffee mornings and even professionally in the BHS staff canteen! After being treated to this sweet coconuty biscuity bake myself since a very young age, the recipe has been passed onto me, and now I get to share it with you. It's an all-time favourite in our house, and I hope this will be the same in your home.

INGREDIENTS

Makes about 24 slices.

120g cornflakes (gf)
200g self-raising flour (gf)
120g desiccated coconut
120g sugar
150g butter
300g icing sugar
3–4 tablespoons water
50g desiccated coconut, for decoration

METHOD

Preheat the oven to 180°C fan/190°C conventional/gas mark 5. Line a Swiss roll tin or roasting tin about 30cm x 20cm with baking paper.

1. Roughly crush the cornflakes into smaller flakes and mix with the flour, coconut and sugar in a large bowl.

2. Melt the butter in a pan and pour onto the dry ingredients in the bowl. Mix until evenly coated.

3. Tightly pack the mixture into the lined tin using the back of a spoon. Bake in the oven for about 15 minutes; it should be lightly golden.

4. While the base is in the oven, mix the icing sugar with the water until you create a smooth fluid, but not overly runny, consistency.

5. Use the icing to cover the cornflake-y base when it is still warm out of the oven and liberally sprinkle desiccated coconut over the top.

6. Leave for a couple of hours to cool and for the icing to set. Then remove from the tin and cut into about 24 pieces.

CHERRY SLICE

The canteen at my high school sold cherry slices at break and lunchtime, and we learned how to make a bake like this in home economics. Everyone loved that class because we all had the best snack for the walk home after school!

This is a no-bake make, and it is incredibly simple and quick to put together. There is no way not to get sticky, though. You need to get a clean hand in there to work it together and inevitably it gets caked in the sticky condensed milk mixture; but that's half the fun! The other half's in the eating.

INGREDIENTS

100g digestive biscuits, crushed
10 glacé cherries, halved
10 large marshmallows, quartered
30g desiccated coconut
25g pistachios, shelled
100g condensed milk

METHOD

1. Mix together the prepared digestives, cherries, marshmallows, desiccated coconut and pistachios in a mixing bowl. Pour in the condensed milk and stir to combine. Leave the mixture aside for about 10 minutes, this will make it easier to shape.

2. Use your hands to press the mixture into a rough log, you have to use quite a bit of force. Lay the log over a large sheet of baking paper or cling film and roll up tightly. Chill in the fridge for at least 30 minutes.

3. Once chilled and set, remove from the fridge and cut into slices as thick as you want!

BLACKBERRY AND ALMOND ETON MESS

Eton mess is more an assembly job rather than baking. Soft cream with sharp berries and crunchy sweet meringue is always a guaranteed winner for a spring or summer dessert. It is best eaten within an hour of making, so the meringue doesn't soften. This is a great reason to get out of helping wash the dishes. Someone else can wash the plates while you make pudding. If all the components are ready to go, it will only take about 5 minutes to put together.

This recipe is simply a guide for what you can do. Blackberry and almond is a great flavour pairing, but this is a brilliant recipe for playing about. Use a different berry or your favourite fruit, ripple some lemon curd through the cream, mix in crushed biscuits rather than meringue, or add toasted oats. The options are as endless as your imagination.

INGREDIENTS

Serves about 6.

40g flaked almonds
80g meringue kisses (shop-bought or use the French meringue recipe on page 25)
300g blackberries
400ml double cream
20g icing sugar
2 teaspoons vanilla bean paste
½ teaspoon almond extract

METHOD

Preheat the oven to 180°C fan/190°C conventional/ gas mark 5.

1. Spread the flaked almonds out on a baking tray and toast in the oven for about 10 minutes, turning halfway. Take the almonds out when they are brown and smell nutty. Leave to cool.

2. Crush the meringue kisses into a rough crumbly texture.

3. Mash half of the blackberries with a fork to create what looks like a rough purée. Slice the remaining blackberries in half.

4. Whip the double cream with the icing sugar, vanilla and almond extract to soft-medium peaks.

5. Gently fold through the flaked almonds, crushed meringue and mashed and halved blackberries. Reserve some halved blackberries and flaked almonds to decorate.

6. Spoon the mixture into serving glasses or bowls and decorate with the reserved blackberries and flaked almonds.

FLAPJACK

Flapjack is one of the first bakes I would make alongside my mum in the kitchen. Mum likes to make crunchy flapjacks, which make excellent tea dunkers if that's your thing. I love my mum's flapjacks; however, I prefer a softer, chewier flapjack, so this recipe combines the two: a crunchy edge with a soft centre. As the flapjack sits, it firms up slightly and the texture moves from being quite crumbly to satisfyingly thick and chewy, so I think it's best to let it sit overnight before digging in.

It's the ultimate break-time snack or packed lunch treat the day after you've baked these. I've also added some roasted nuts to add a different layer of flavour and texture, but feel free to omit these.

INGREDIENTS

100g nuts of your choice (optional)
300g butter
200g golden syrup
100g light brown sugar
400g rolled oats (gf)
50g self-raising flour (gf)
1 teaspoon salt

METHOD

Preheat the oven to 160°C fan/170°C conventional/ gas mark 3.5. Grease and line a 20cm square tin.

1. Place the nuts on a baking tray and roast for 10 to 15 minutes or until golden and smelling toasty and nutty. Leave to cool, then roughly chop.

2. Melt together the butter, syrup and sugar in a pan over a medium heat until just melted. Mix together the oats, flour, salt, and chopped roasted nuts in a large bowl, then pour over the melted butter mixture and stir until all the ingredients are coated evenly.

3. Pour this mixture into the lined tin. Compress the mix firmly by pressing down with the back of a spoon. Bake for 40 to 45 minutes or until deeply golden all over.

4. Leave to cool in the tin, then remove and slice into 9 or 16 squares.

PEANUT BUTTER COOKIES

My friends have been helping me out by taste testing as I create the recipes for this book. And this is one of the bakes that they've liked best out of all of them. Part of me is almost annoyed about this because it is such a simple recipe that didn't take a huge amount of time to devise. But sometimes this is the way. Simple bakes with few ingredients can be just as good, if not even better, than more complicated ones.

INGREDIENTS

200g light brown sugar
200g peanut butter, smooth or crunchy
1 teaspoon bicarbonate of soda
½ teaspoon salt
1 large egg
80g chocolate chips, milk or dark as you prefer

METHOD

Preheat the oven to 160°C fan/170°C conventional/ gas mark 3.5. Line two baking trays with baking paper.

1. Add the sugar, peanut butter, bicarbonate of soda, salt and egg into a bowl and mix until combined. This is easiest with an electric hand mixer. Throw in the chocolate chips and stir through.

2. Roll into 12 balls and place these on the baking trays, leaving a good amount of space between each ball. Sometimes the chocolate chips will fall out of the stiff dough. Just press them back into the balls on the tray. Flatten the balls with the palm of your hand and bake for 10 to 12 minutes, until beginning to brown around the edges.

BROWNIES

When my family ask for brownies, they don't want anything fancy; they simply want a fudgy square of chocolatey goodness. This is just that: a simple brownie recipe that comes out satisfyingly dense and fudgy with a rich chocolate flavour.

However, there is one slightly intriguing addition to this brownie . . . the dates. I think these are brilliant. Their amazing sticky quality enhances the fudgy texture, and they add a gentle caramel note to the flavour. Unless you know they are in the recipe, you wouldn't be able to tell the brownies had dates in them, but I will forgive you if you really don't want to add them!

INGREDIENTS

130g butter
130g dark chocolate (I use 55% chocolate)
90g caster sugar
90g dark brown sugar
2 large eggs
100g plain flour (gf + ½ teaspoon xanthan gum)
35g cocoa powder
½ teaspoon salt
40g dates, chopped
1 teaspoon vanilla bean paste

METHOD

Preheat the oven to 170°C fan/180°C conventional/gas mark 4. Grease and base line a 20cm square cake tin.

1. Melt the butter, chocolate, caster sugar and brown sugar in a large bowl over a pan of simmering water.

2. Once melted, leave to cool for a few minutes, then whisk in the eggs. Sieve over the flour and cocoa powder and stir through along with the salt, dates and vanilla.

3. Pour the smooth, shiny batter into the tin and level off. Bake for about 25 minutes until a thin layer of moist crumbs and batter remain on a skewer inserted into the middle of the brownie, and you can hear it gently bubble slightly louder than a regular sponge.

4. Leave to cool in the tin. Then – if you can resist eating them straight away – place into the fridge for at least an hour before slicing into 9 squares.

TRIPLE CHOCOLATE TRUFFLES

Truffles are the most ridiculously easy sweet to make but can also look quite fancy and impressive when you serve them. The coverings that go around the truffles are there to stop them from being too messy to eat. You have free rein to choose any covering you want. Be sure to chop it quite fine so it covers the truffles well. Chopped nuts, cocoa powder or even blitzed breakfast cereal will all work well.

INGREDIENTS

For dark chocolate truffles
100g double cream
75g dark chocolate

For milk chocolate truffles
100g double cream
100g milk chocolate

For white chocolate truffles
100g double cream
150g white chocolate

To decorate – you choose!
50g pistachios, chopped
10g freeze-dried raspberry pieces
15g cocoa powder

METHOD

1. Heat the cream in a pan until it just begins to bubble. Remove from the heat and stir in the chocolate of your choice, broken into chunks. It will look split at first but keep gently stirring until it is smooth.

2. Leave to chill in the fridge for at least 2 hours to set.

3. Cover a plate or small bowl with the covering of your choice.

4. Scoop a teaspoon of the set mixture and roll it into a ball in your hands. The outside of the truffle will melt slightly in the heat of your hands. Roll the truffle in the coating to cover. Leave aside to set again. Repeat with the coverings of your choice until all your truffle mix is used. Beware: things could turn messy!

5. Leave at room temperature for a soft truffle. For a firmer truffle, eat fridge cold.

HONEYCOMB

It's pure science, of course, but making honeycomb feels like magic. The way the mixture foams and bubbles up after you add in the bicarbonate of soda is still wildly exciting every time I do it. The mixture rises because of the carbon dioxide being released from the bicarbonate of soda. The mixture cools and sets around the trapped bubbles of carbon dioxide resulting in the beautiful honeycomb texture you see when you break into the candy.

The sugar has to reach 150°C, which is incredibly hot, so be very careful with this stage. This part definitely needs adult supervision; best to not have little hands do this alone. It's a good idea to have a bowl of cold water on your workstation in case any hot mixture spits onto your hands.

INGREDIENTS

100g caster sugar
50g golden syrup
1 teaspoon bicarbonate of soda
200g dark chocolate (optional)

METHOD

Line a small roasting tin with non-stick baking paper.

1. Mix the sugar and syrup in a high-sided pan over high heat until the sugar has dissolved and it begins to bubble.

2. Continue heating the sugar until the mixture looks and smells a deep caramel or registers 150°C on a sugar thermometer. Remove this from the heat, quickly throw in the bicarbonate of soda and stir until combined. The mixture will bubble up and look foamy.

3. Quickly pour the mixture out into the lined tin and leave to cool at room temperature.

4. Once cool and hardened, break into large chunks using your hands.

5. To create chocolate honeycomb, melt 150g of chocolate in the microwave, then stir through the remaining 50g of chocolate until melted. Dip the honeycomb chunks into the melted chocolate. Encourage the excess chocolate to drip off and then leave to set at room temperature on some baking paper.

CHAPTER 8
CHRISTMAS

If you watched the *Great British Bake Off*, you might have noticed that I am quite a fan of Christmas. It is my favourite time of year to hunker down in a cosy kitchen when it's cold and dark outside. It's also the perfect time to share baking with friends and family, whether as gifts or to welcome them in as a festive host. These are some of my best-loved festive recipes that I make around the holidays, and I hope they will become among your favourites too.

PUFF PASTRY MINCE PIES

INGREDIENTS

For the mincemeat

400g mincemeat, shop-
    bought is fine
1 medium eating apple,
    peeled, cored and diced
    small
80g dried cranberries

For the pastry

1 quantity rough puff pastry
    (page 14)
1 egg, beaten

Portuguese custard tarts, *pastel de nata,* have a fantastic pastry case made of rolled-up puff pastry, which creates flaky rings of pastry on the underside of the tarts. I think this style of pastry makes for a welcome upgrade for mince pies. I first made mince pies like this a few Christmases ago, but I made the rookie error of not baking the pies with the muffin tin inside another baking tray. As a result, a fair amount of butter leakage occurred, and as it burned on the oven base it created rather a lot of smoke! So, this recipe comes with a big recommend, but I also strongly recommend you use a rimmed baking tray to catch any potential butter leakage!

METHOD

Preheat the oven to 200°C fan/
210°C conventional/gas mark 7.
You will need a 12-hole muffin tin.

Make the mincemeat

1. Stir the diced apples and the cranberries through the mincemeat and set aside.

Assemble and bake the pies

1. Make the puff pastry as instructed on page 14. Then roll out two thirds of it on a lightly floured surface into a rough rectangle about 12cm x 30cm. Tightly roll up the pastry into a log, like a Swiss roll, from one of the short sides. Tightly wrap this in cling film and chill in the fridge for at least 30 minutes.

2. Cut the dough roll into 12 equal slices. Place a slice, cut side down, into each hole of your muffin tin. Lightly wet your thumbs and use them to press the pastry into the corner of the tin and ease it up the sides just above the top of the moulds.

3. Fill each pastry case with a heaped tablespoon of the mincemeat mix, so it sits just below the top of the pastry.

4. Roll the remaining one third of dough out to about ¼ cm thick. Cut 12 circles from the dough, the same size as the muffin tin openings. Brush the top edges of the pastry cases with a little egg wash before laying over a pastry circle lid. Firmly press the lid onto the pastry cases to join using a fork or your fingers. Cut a small hole in the top of the pastry lids. Use a pastry brush to brush the lids with egg wash.

5. Place the muffin tin in a large rimmed tray to catch any leaking butter. Bake for about 25 minutes or until deeply golden. Leave to cool for about 5 minutes before removing from the tin and cooling further on a wire rack.

MINCE PIE BAKEWELL TART

INGREDIENTS

For the pastry
1 quantity sweet shortcrust
  pastry (page 18) (gf)
1 teaspoon ground
  cinnamon

For the mincemeat
175g mincemeat
½ eating apple, peeled,
  cored and diced small
30g dried cranberries

For the frangipane
100g butter, softened
100g light brown sugar
75g self-raising flour (gf)
2 large eggs
125g ground almonds
½ teaspoon ground ginger
½ teaspoon ground
  cinnamon
½ teaspoon ground mixed
  spice
¼ teaspoon salt

To assemble and ice
20g mixed peel (plus extra
  for topping)
25g icing sugar
1 teaspoon brandy

This is a bit of a change-up for a dessert to enjoy during the festive period. It has all the classic Christmas flavours but wrapped up in a form that is just a little different for the season. I use shop-bought mincemeat; I know many people say homemade tastes better, and I'm sure it does, but this is a shortcut I always make. However, I like to add fresh apple and dried cranberries to spike the shop-bought mincemeat and make it fresher and more special.

METHOD

Preheat the oven to 180°C fan/
190°C conventional/gas mark 5.

Make the pastry
1. Make and blind bake a 20–23cm
   shortcrust pastry case as instructed
   on page 18. When making the
   pastry, add 1 teaspoon ground
   cinnamon into the dough along
   with the flour.

Reduce the oven to 160°C fan/
170°C conventional/gas mark 3.5.

Mix the mincemeat
1. Stir the chopped apple and
   dried cranberries through the
   mincemeat. Optionally you can
   simply use 275g mincemeat
   without the add-ins.

Make the frangipane
1. Cream together the butter and
   sugar until light and fluffy (this
   will take 3 to 5 minutes with an
   electric mixer).

2. Add in the flour, eggs, ground
   almonds, spices and salt, then mix
   until combined.

Assemble and bake the tart
1. Spread the mincemeat over the
   base of the pastry case. Top this
   with the frangipane and level off;
   this is most easily done by piping
   over and spreading out with a
   palette knife or spoon. Sprinkle the
   mixed peel over the frangipane.
   Bake in the oven for about 35
   minutes until the frangipane feels
   set in the centre when gently
   pressed with your finger. Remove
   from the tin to cool on a wire rack.

2. Make the icing by mixing the icing
   sugar with the brandy until you
   achieve a thick fluid consistency.
   Then drizzle the icing over the top
   of the cooled tart from a spoon
   with bold strokes. Top the icing
   with a little more mixed peel.

GINGERBREAD FUDGE

INGREDIENTS

1 tin condensed milk
  (about 400g)
200ml milk
450g dark brown sugar
100g butter
1 teaspoon ground ginger
1 teaspoon ground
  cinnamon
½ teaspoon ground mixed
  spice
½ teaspoon salt
75g pistachios, roughly
  chopped
50g dried cranberries
20g white chocolate

Especially around the festive period, it's nice to have baking in the tins, ready to give away as a gift or to set out with a cup of tea for any visitors. Fudge is the perfect 'for the tins' bake as it keeps so well and you can make it well ahead of time. Wrapping squares of this fudge in cellophane or a paper bag with a nice ribbon makes a rather lovely gift for friends and family. This recipe is classically sweet and rich, but with warming winter spices and caramelly flavours to make it a Christmas treat.

METHOD

Line a 20cm square cake tin with baking paper.

1. Add the condensed milk, milk, sugar, butter, spices and salt into a high-sided non-stick pan. Place over a medium heat, stirring until everything has melted and the mixture is smooth.

2. Increase to a high heat and bubble away for about 10 minutes, frequently stirring to prevent sticking, or until the mixture registers 112–115°C on a sugar thermometer.

3. Remove from the heat and leave to cool for about 3 minutes. Beat the mixture for a couple of minutes until it thickens slightly and pulls away from the side of the pan while beating, but is still smooth, fluid and shiny. Add in the pistachios and dried cranberries, reserving about a fifth of them for decoration. Stir through, then pour the mixture into the prepared tin.

4. Leave to set firm at room temperature, for at least 2 hours.

5. Use a sharp knife to cut the fudge into small squares but leave them locked together as one large piece. Now melt the white chocolate, drizzle it over the fudge from a height, and then sprinkle over the remaining pistachios and cranberries.

6. Leave the chocolate to set before separating the squares of fudge.

PISTACHIO, ALMOND AND CRANBERRY NOUGAT

INGREDIENTS

Icing sugar, for dusting
100g pistachios
100g almonds
350g caster sugar
100g golden syrup
150g clear honey
50ml water
2 large egg whites
½ teaspoon salt
100g dried cranberries

This is another excellent bake to fill the tins or to give away as a little festive gift. The cranberries and nuts look like jewels sitting in the nougat and make the entire decoration with very little input required from you. Nougat is quite simple to make; however, it does require a stand mixer when whisking the egg whites and sugar syrup. An electric hand whisk could easily get clogged up and would take quite a while longer.

METHOD

Preheat the oven to 170°C fan/ 180°C conventional/gas mark 4. Line the base and sides of a 20cm square tin with non-stick baking paper. Dust the paper with a thick layer of icing sugar.

1. Roast the pistachios and almonds in the oven for about 10 minutes until golden and smelling toasty.

2. Add the sugar, golden syrup, honey and water into a large pan over a high heat. Stir until the sugar has dissolved and the mixture begins to boil. You can continue to stir this as it bubbles without it crystallising thanks to the addition of golden syrup.

3. Meanwhile, gently whisk the egg whites in the bowl of a stand mixer with the salt until it takes on a cloud-like texture.

4. Remove the sugar mixture from the heat once it reaches 145°C. Slowly pour this mixture into the egg whites while mixing at high speed. Whisk on high speed until the mixture is thick and shiny but still slightly warm; this will take about 5 to 10 minutes.

5. Add the roasted nuts and cranberries and stir through the thick mixture until evenly dispersed. Pour the mixture into the lined tin. Cut another sheet of baking paper to the size of the tin, press onto the nougat and flatten out. The easiest way to do this is to press the same size cake tin onto the baking paper.

6. Leave the nougat to cool and set at room temperature for a couple of hours or overnight. Remove from the tin, peel off the top layer of baking paper but leave on the bottom layer. Cover the top of the nougat with a heavy dusting of icing sugar. Use a sharp knife to cut into small portions and then peel off the bottom paper from the small pieces.

PENGUIN CAKES

INGREDIENTS

For the cakes
175g butter, softened
175g caster sugar
3 large eggs
175g self-raising flour (gf)
30g freeze-dried raspberry
    powder (optional)
1 teaspoon baking powder
    (gf)
½ teaspoon salt
3 tablespoons milk

For the buttercream
100g butter, softened
½ teaspoon salt
150g icing sugar
1 teaspoon vanilla extract
Orange gel food colouring

To decorate
300g black fondant icing
Icing sugar and cornflour,
    for rolling

I'm not very good at intricate cake decorating and making life-like novelty cakes, so that's why I keep the design simple when making shaped cakes like these. These little penguin cakes require minimal moulding or shaping and have very few details, but still achieve the goal of being cute and fun. The sponge itself is a delicious raspberry flavour for no particular reason, which means you can always omit the freeze-dried raspberry and add 1½ teaspoons of flavour extract and some zest or other flavouring of your choice.

METHOD

Preheat the oven to 170°C fan/180°C conventional/gas mark 4. Grease 6 dariole moulds with butter, and line the base with a small circle of non-stick baking paper.

Make the cakes
1. Cream together the butter and sugar with an electric hand whisk or stand mixer until light and fluffy; this will take 3 to 5 minutes.

2. Add in the eggs, flour, raspberry powder, baking powder, salt and milk. Stir until fully combined into the cake batter.

3. Split the mixture evenly between the 6 moulds; this is easiest with a piping bag. Level off the tops of the cakes and bake for 20 to 25 minutes or until a skewer inserted into the centre comes out clean; you will hear a gentle bubble and the cakes will begin to pull away from the side of the tin.

4. Allow to cool for 5 minutes in the moulds before turning out and cooling completely on a wire rack.

Make the buttercream
1. Cream the butter and salt with an electric hand whisk or stand mixer until considerably lightened in colour; this takes about 3 minutes.

2. Add in 50g of icing sugar and beat into the butter on high speed for a minute or two until it is feeling very light and smooth. Repeat this until you have used all the icing sugar. Mix through the vanilla extract.

3. Put a fifth of the buttercream into a separate bowl and colour orange with a little of the food colouring.

4. Cover and set the buttercreams aside at room temperature.

Decorate your penguins
1. Use a palette knife to spread a thin layer of white buttercream around the sponges.

2. Knead the black fondant for a couple of minutes until soft and pliable. Roll out about a quarter of the fondant on a surface lightly dusted with a 50:50 mixture of cornflour and icing sugar until you have a circle about 18cm in diameter and about ¼ cm thick.

Continues overleaf . . .

3. Lift up the fondant and drape it over an iced sponge. Gently press the fondant down the sides of the sponge, unfurling any pleats at the bottom while working the fondant down the cake. Trim the excess fondant away from the base of the cake.

4. Repeat the process of rolling and covering for the rest of the cakes.

5. Fill 2 piping bags with the remaining white buttercream and orange buttercream.

6. Pipe a tall rectangle of white buttercream with a domed top from the bottom centre of the front of the cake to create the penguin's belly. Pipe 2 circles of white buttercream towards the top of the cakes to make the penguin's eyes. Roll 2 small balls of black fondant and press them into the eyes.

7. Pipe a small orange buttercream triangle for the beak at the top of the belly. Pipe on orange flippers at the bottom sides of the belly.

MINI GINGERBREAD HOUSES

INGREDIENTS

For the templates
Cereal boxes or other card

For the gingerbread
175g butter
125g dark muscovado sugar
100g golden syrup
450g plain flour (gf +
    ¾ teaspoon xanthan gum)
1½ teaspoons bicarbonate
    of soda
½ teaspoon salt
2 teaspoons ground ginger
2 teaspoons ground
    cinnamon
1 teaspoon ground nutmeg

For the royal icing
80g pasteurised egg whites
    (or 2 large egg whites)
2 teaspoons lemon juice
420g icing sugar
Green gel food colouring

To decorate
Christmas sprinkles (optional)
    (ensure gf)

My mum connects the time I first made a gingerbread house by myself on a random December morning when I was 13 with her realisation of how baking-mad I am. When I was 15, I made a template for these mini gingerbread houses and sold them for a charity bake sale. They were quite a hit and made a nice festive decoration in people's kitchens before being enjoyed as a tasty treat later. This recipe was also the first video I put up on my YouTube channel, which continues to be a source of cringy entertainment for my flatmates! This recipe will make 4 houses.

METHOD

Preheat the oven to 180°C fan/ 190°C conventional/gas mark 5. Line 2 baking trays with non-stick baking paper.

Cut the templates for the gingerbread houses out of card:

- Roof: 11cm x 6cm rectangle

- Sides: 8cm x 6cm rectangle

- Front and back: 8cm x 6cm rectangle with a 3cm tall isosceles triangle on top. Draw a line 3cm up from the centre of an 8cm side. Draw lines attaching the point of this line to the corners of the 8cm side.

- Four 12cm x 11cm cardboard rectangles, covered in silver foil to make bases for the houses.

Make the gingerbread
1. Add the butter, sugar and syrup into a pan over a low heat. Stir occasionally until the butter has melted and all the sugar has dissolved.

2. Meanwhile, add all the remaining ingredients into a large mixing bowl and stir to combine. Add in the liquid sugar and butter mixture and stir into the dry mix until all the flour has been incorporated.

3. Allow to cool until barely warm to the touch, then tip out onto your work surface and knead for a couple of minutes until smooth and shiny. Split the mixture into 2 portions and wrap in cling film.

4. Take one of the portions of dough and roll out on a lightly floured board to about ¾ cm thick. Cut out 4 of each template. Cut a small 2cm wide x 3.5cm tall rectangle from the bottom centre of two of the fronts to make the doors for the houses. Place these on lined baking trays, with a little space in between pieces and bake for 7 to 10 minutes or until browning gently around the edges.

5. Repeat this process for the second half of dough. You can re-roll any offcuts. In total, you should have 8 biscuits of each template shape.

Make the royal icing
1. Whisk the egg whites until frothy. Add in the lemon juice and whisk in the icing sugar in 4 batches. This is best done with an electric hand whisk or stand mixer.

Continues overleaf . . .

MINI GINGERBREAD HOUSES
CONTINUED

2. The mixture should be firm, shiny and able to hold its shape. Fill a piping bag fitted with a small round nozzle or a plain piping bag, then cut a small hole.

Assemble the houses

1. Pipe a border of royal icing around the door frames and pipe windows onto the front, sides and back of the houses.

2. Spread a layer of icing around the border of the serving boards and pat with a palette knife or spoon to create a snowy look.

3. Pipe royal icing onto the bottom edge of a house front and press this down on the serving board. Pipe down one of the inside edges and press a house side with royal icing piped onto its bottom edge into this to join. Repeat this with the other side of the house and pipe down the open edges of the sides and attach the back of the house. Leave this to set for about 30 minutes while you repeat this process with the remaining houses.

4. Pipe royal icing down the slanted sides of the front and back of the houses and attach the roof pieces to these. The roof should slightly overhang the front, back and sides of the house.

5. Pipe royal icing along all of the open edges of the roof to look like snow. Use a toothpick to ruffle these royal icing borders and give texture.

6. Pipe out the remaining icing and colour green with a little gel food colouring. Add to a piping bag fitted with a closed star nozzle and pipe vertically, directly up at the front of the gingerbread house to create a Christmas tree. Sprinkle some Christmas sprinkles over the trees.

7. Liberally dust icing sugar over the houses before staging your own gingerbread village!

CHRISTMAS PUDDING

INGREDIENTS

For the pudding

85g plain flour (gf + pinch xanthan gum)
1 teaspoon ground mixed spice
½ teaspoon ground ginger
½ teaspoon ground cinnamon
¼ teaspoon ground nutmeg
90g suet or vegetable suet
50g dark muscovado sugar
50g breadcrumbs (gf)
100g blanched almonds
50g glacé cherries, halved
25g candied mixed peel
1 orange, zested and juiced
1 lemon, zested and juiced
1 cooking apple, peeled, cored and coarsely grated
450g dried mixed fruit
2 large eggs
70ml cider

For the brandy butter

150g butter, softened
100g icing sugar
½ teaspoon salt
3–5 tablespoons brandy

To serve

2 tablespoons brandy

In our house, Christmas day is not complete without Mum's homemade Christmas pudding. I tend to make an alternative dessert, but it's never devoured as quickly as the pudding. Super rich, packed with fruit, nuts and warm spices, it's really very special. For me, the most fun moment of Christmas dinner is is dimming the lights and setting the pudding ablaze!

METHOD

Grease a 1 litre or 2 pint pudding basin with butter.

Make the pudding

1. Add all the ingredients from the flour to the candied mixed peel into a large mixing bowl and stir until everything is evenly coated in flour. Add in all the remaining ingredients and stir until combined in a thick batter consistency.

2. Put the mixture into the pudding basin, pack down tightly and level off on top.

3. If using a plastic pudding basin, grease the inside of the lid and clip into place. If not, cut a circle of both baking paper and foil about 10cm larger than the basin. Place the baking paper over the basin and cover with the foil, and tuck around the basin. Tie the foil around the basin with string. Fold a sheet of foil 4 times lengthways to create a long, strong strip. Place the pudding basin onto this, using it as a handle.

4. Place a small upturned plate into the base of a large pan. Sit the basin onto the plate and fill around with boiling water reaching 2cm up the side of the basin. Place a lid on the pan and gently simmer on a low heat for 4 hours to steam the pudding. Check the water level every now and then so the pan doesn't run dry.

5. Remove from the pan and leave to cool. Cover the surface with a fresh piece of baking paper and cover that with cling film. Thus we would store this pudding happily for over a year.

6. When ready to serve, reheat the pudding by steaming it for about an hour or heat it in the microwave for about 10 minutes.

Make the brandy butter

1. Cream the butter with an electric hand whisk or stand mixer for a few minutes until very light in texture and colour. Add in the icing sugar 2 tablespoons at a time and beat in for a couple of minutes after each addition until light and smooth.

2. Once you have added all the sugar, add the salt and beat in with the brandy a tablespoon at a time. Taste the mixture as you add the brandy until you are happy with the flavour. Serve alongside the Christmas pudding.

To serve

1. When everything's ready, gently warm the brandy until you see the first signs of steaming vapour. Pour the brandy over the pudding and carefully light with a long match, before bringing to the table while gently shaking and moving the plate to keep the flames burning.

CHRISTMAS PUDDING ICE CREAM BOMBS

INGREDIENTS

For the ice cream
500ml milk
250ml double cream
6 large egg yolks
140g dark muscovado sugar
1 teaspoon vanilla extract
1 teaspoon flaky salt
250g Christmas pudding/
    Christmas cake off-cuts
    (page 231/235), chilled
    in the fridge

To decorate
400g dark chocolate
50g marzipan (page 235)
Green gel food colouring
Red gel food colouring
Cornflour and icing sugar,
    for rolling
75g white chocolate

Ice cream is good every time of the year, and Christmas is no exception. I love this recipe, which is very rich and slightly caramelly, but you can simply mix some Christmas cake or pudding through softened shop-bought ice cream if you want to skip a step. However, take your time and make sure the ice creams are frozen solid before dipping and coating, or it can quickly become a sticky mess.

METHOD

Make the ice cream

1. Heat the milk and cream in a pan, occasionally stirring, until it reaches a boil. Whisk together the egg yolks, sugar and vanilla.

2. Pour the hot milk and cream over the egg yolk mix, whisking constantly. Return this mixture to the pan over a low heat, continually stirring until the custard has thickened to thickly coat the back of a spoon and bubbles have subsided (75–82°C).

3. Transfer to a shallow tray, cover the surface with cling film or baking paper and chill until fridge cold.

4. Once the mixture is cold, churn it in an ice cream machine (or see other methods on page 50) until it looks like soft-serve ice cream. At this stage, add in the flaky salt, and crumble the Christmas pudding or Christmas cake into the mixture and mix through.

Shape the ice cream bombs

1. Fill silicone hemisphere moulds with the soft-serve textured ice cream. The hemispheres can be as big or small as you like (this recipe fills 12 hemispheres of 6cm). Spread away excess ice cream from the top and place in the freezer for at least 3 hours until completely frozen.

2. Gently heat an empty saucepan on the hob, then turn it upside down. Take a solid ice cream half out from a mould and gently melt the flat side by running it over the warm flat underside of the pan. Press this into the flat side of another hemisphere to fuse. Use your hands to smooth out the join and place the sphere back into a mould and back into the freezer. Repeat this for all the remaining hemispheres.

3. Melt the dark chocolate in the microwave or a bowl over simmering water, so it is fully melted and quite fluid. Pour into a deep mug or jug that is wider than the ice cream domes.

Continues overleaf . . .

4. Press a fork into the top of a completely frozen ice cream sphere and dunk into the melted chocolate. The chocolate will freeze around the ice cream. Quickly remove the bomb from the chocolate, place it on a baking tray, and back into the freezer. It is okay for there to be a little ice cream peeking through the chocolate at the top.

Decorate the ice cream bombs

1. Split the marzipan into 2 portions, one with two thirds of the marzipan and the other with one third. Colour the larger portion by kneading through green gel food colouring until you achieve a leaf-like colour. Colour the other portion a deep red by kneading through red gel food colouring.

2. Roll out the green marzipan on a surface dusted with a little cornflour and icing sugar until about ¼ cm thick. Cut out holly leaves using a holly plunger cutter.

3. Roll tiny balls from the red marzipan. Brush a little water over the marzipan leaves and attach three red balls on top to make it look like holly.

4. Melt the white chocolate and fill a piping bag with this.

5. Remove the ice cream bombs from the freezer. Pipe the white chocolate over the top of the ice cream bombs. The chocolate will freeze onto the bombs very fast, so pipe down the sides a little to make it look as though the chocolate has dripped down from the top.

6. Top the white chocolate with your marzipan holly and put back in the freezer until nearly ready to serve – you'll need to remove them from the freezer about 10 to 15 minutes before serving.

CHRISTMAS CAKE

INGREDIENTS

For the cake
800g dried mixed fruit
200g dates, roughly chopped
120ml brandy or whisky
1 orange, zested and juiced
1 lemon, zested and juiced
250g butter, softened
250g dark muscovado sugar
350g plain flour (gf + ¼
  teaspoon xanthan gum)
1 teaspoon mixed spice
1 teaspoon ground cinnamon
¼ teaspoon ground ginger
¼ teaspoon ground nutmeg
3 large eggs
100g glacé cherries, halved
100g candied mixed peel
100g blanched almonds
2 tablespoons additional
  brandy or whisky

For the marzipan
400g ground almonds
200g icing sugar
200g caster sugar
140–160g pasteurised whole
  egg (or 2–2.5 large eggs)
Icing sugar and cornflour, for
  rolling out
50g apricot jam

For the royal icing
120g pasteurised egg white
  (or 3 large egg whites)
600g icing sugar
2 teaspoons lemon juice

To decorate
1 egg white
6 rosemary stalks
20g granulated sugar
50g fresh or dried
  cranberries
6 cinnamon sticks
6 whole star anise
2 oranges, thinly sliced and
  dried in a 90°C oven for
  at least 90 minutes.

The first Christmas when my folks were married, my mum started making Christmas pudding and Christmas cake from the November 1993 BBC *Good Food* magazine. Every year since she has continued this, although there is now quite a lot of scribbling and amendments in the margins as Mum's refined the recipes. Over the past few years, I have respectfully changed up Mum's changed-up recipe to lean into what I like from a Christmas cake, and this is that.

I include a marzipan recipe here. You can use shop-bought marzipan, but it is honestly so easy to make, and so worthwhile for the best taste and quality.

METHOD

Prepare the fruit

1. Place the dried mixed fruit and dates in a bowl, then stir in the brandy or whisky, plus the orange and lemon zest and juice. Cover the bowl and leave to sit for at least 12 hours or overnight.

2. When the fruit is ready for you to start making the cake, preheat the oven to 140°C fan/150°C conventional/gas mark 2. Grease and line a deep 23cm cake tin with baking paper. Cut a strip of baking paper at least 75cm long and 4cm wider than the height of your tin. Fold a 2cm flap along the length of the strip and make slanted cuts periodically along the flap. Fit this around the sides of the tin. Cut a circle of baking paper and fit this to the base of the tin.

Make the cake

1. Cream together the butter and sugar until light and fluffy, this will take 3 to 5 minutes with an electric mixer. Add all remaining cake ingredients, including the soaked fruit (but not the additional brandy or whisky), and mix until the batter is smooth and the fruit and nuts are evenly suspended.

2. Transfer the batter to the prepared cake tin and smooth out the top. Bake for 2 hours 30 minutes to 2 hours 45 minutes, until a skewer comes out clean from the centre. Watch to see if the cake browns too quickly; if it does, then loosely cover the tin with foil to avoid the top burning.

3. Leave the cake to cool in the tin.

4. Once cooled, use a skewer to poke holes all over the cake and pour over the additional brandy or whisky and leave to soak in.

5. You can ice and eat this cake straight away, but if you'd like to keep the cake for a couple of months before icing, wrap it in a clean layer of baking paper followed by a tight layer of cling film or foil. Remove the cake from the wrapping every 3 to 5 weeks and feed it by drizzling over an additional 2 tablespoons of the spirit of your choice.

Continues overleaf . . .

Make the marzipan

1. Mix the ground almonds, icing sugar and caster sugar. Beat the egg and add it gradually, mixing with a knife, then kneading with your hands to make a pliable but not overly sticky dough. If too wet, add more almonds, icing sugar and caster sugar in the ratio 2:1:1. If too dry, it won't roll out, so add in a splash of water. Cover in cling film and chill for at least an hour.

2. Boil the apricot jam in a small pan and pass through a sieve.

3. Carefully trim the top of the cake to make it flat. Place this upside down onto your serving plate, so the bottom of the cake with a sharp corner is now the top. Use a pastry brush to brush a thin layer of the apricot jam over the cake.

4. Roll out the marzipan on a surface dusted with a 50:50 mix of cornflour and icing sugar into a rough circle 38cm in diameter. Cut off any jagged edges from the marzipan and roll back over your rolling pin.

5. Lift up the marzipan and roll it back out, draping it over the cake. Gently press it down the sides of the cake, working from the top. Unfurl the pleats of marzipan at the bottom of the cake and press the marzipan flush against the cake. Repeat the process of unfurling pleats and pressing down onto the cake. It doesn't matter if the marzipan cracks, as it will be covered in icing. Run a knife around the base edge of the cake to cut away any excess marzipan.

6. You can use any offcuts to make decorative holly (from the ice cream bombs on page 233) or marzipan fruits for the top of the cake.

Make the royal icing

1. Put the egg whites, icing sugar and lemon juice in a stand mixer with a whisk attachment. Mix on low speed to combine, then kick up to high speed and whisk for 2 to 3 minutes. It should be shiny and stiff but spreadable. If the icing looks too thick, add in water a teaspoon at a time until it is a spreadable consistency. If the icing is too loose to spread, add more icing sugar.

2. Use a palette knife to spread the royal icing over the marzipan. I like to leave a good amount of texture in the finish by icing with many small swipes instead of one consistent swipe around the cake.

Decorate the cake

1. Lightly beat the egg white, then brush a thin layer of it over the rosemary. Leave aside to dry for about 15 minutes until just slightly tacky to the touch. Sprinkle over granulated sugar to create a frosted effect. Roll the cranberries in the excess sugar that falls from the rosemary.

2. Decorate the cake with a wreath of the frosted rosemary and cranberries, whole spices and dried orange slices.

SPICED CLEMENTINE CAKE

INGREDIENTS

For the cake

5 clementines
5 large eggs
225g caster sugar
125ml olive oil
200g ground almonds
125g self-raising flour (gf)
¾ teaspoon ground
    cinnamon
¾ teaspoon mixed spice
1½ teaspoons baking
    powder (gf)

For the frosting

100g butter, softened
200g icing sugar
200g cream cheese, at
    room temperature

For the filling

200g marmalade

To decorate

1 egg white
20g granulated sugar
6 rosemary stalks
50g fresh or dried
    cranberries
6 cinnamon sticks
6 whole star anise
2 oranges, thinly sliced and
    dried in a 90°C oven for
    at least 90 minutes.

Some people don't love a rich fruit cake, so this recipe is designed to be an alternative that you can bake for anyone who isn't in the fruit cake camp. It is incredibly moist and soft and will keep very well for about 5 days, helped by the addition of oil and ground almonds. It is still festive with the clementine and spice flavours, but is also a little lighter and fresher in texture and flavour than a heavy fruitcake, so it could be a nice change.

METHOD

Preheat the oven to 160°C fan/ 170°C conventional/gas mark 3. Grease and base line 2 x 18cm cake tins.

Make the cake

1. Place the whole clementines in a saucepan with a lid. Cover with water and simmer for 15 to 25 minutes until very soft. Drain the fruit, slice them in half and discard any pips. Leave to cool.

2. Whisk together the eggs and sugar in a stand mixer until light and foamy, not taking the mix all the way to ribbon stage. Stream in the oil while still whisking.

3. Blitz the cooled clementines in a food processor to create a chunky purée. Add 250g of the purée to your egg and sugar mix, along with the ground almonds. Now sieve over the flour, spices and baking powder and fold through. You don't have to be overly gentle here.

4. Evenly split the mix between the prepared tins. Bake for 35 to 40 minutes until it passes the skewer test and the cake has a gentle bubble when you listen to it.

5. Allow to cool in the tins for 10 to 15 minutes, then remove and cool fully on a wire rack.

Make the frosting

1. Beat the butter using an electric hand whisk or stand mixer until smooth and light. Add in the icing sugar in 4 to 6 batches, beating on high speed for 2 minutes after each addition. The mixture should be very light and creamy.

2. Add the cream cheese about 50g at a time, mixing through gently and briefly until just combined after each addition.

Assemble the cake

1. Slice the cooled cakes in half, so you create 4 layers of sponge. Lay one sponge onto your serving plate, and be sure to set aside one of the bases of the cakes with a clean corner to use as your top layer of sponge.

2. Spread a thin layer of marmalade over the sponge and stack with the next layer of sponge. Repeat this using the other three layers of sponge. When you get to the top, stack your final layer so the clean edge is facing up.

3. Dirty ice the cake with a very thin layer of the frosting and chill in the fridge for about 30 minutes.

4. Take from the fridge and spread the remaining frosting over the cake using a palette knife to create swipes and swooshes.

5. Decorate with a sweeping pattern of the same decorations as for the Christmas cake on page 235.

YULE LOG

INGREDIENTS

For the sponge
4 large eggs
110g caster sugar
75g self-raising flour (gf)
35g cocoa powder, plus
    extra for dusting

For the ganache
300g double cream
225g dark chocolate

For the filling
150ml double cream
15g icing sugar
1½ teaspoons vanilla bean
    paste

To decorate
Chopped nuts
Dried fruit
Candied peel (page 48)
Icing sugar, for dusting

I will typically make about 3 yule logs each year because my brother loves them so much! His idea of the perfect cake is vanilla or chocolate, with whipped cream and possibly ganache, nothing fancier. Yule log ticks those boxes, and I don't try to fill it with anything different because I know he'll not enjoy it as much. The other great thing about this is how fast it can all come together. Because the sponge is so quick to bake and cool, I've been able to get a yule log on the table in under an hour from start to finish.

METHOD

Preheat the oven to 170°C fan/ 180°C conventional/gas mark 4. Grease and line a 22cm x 33cm Swiss roll tin.

Make the sponge
1. Make a Swiss roll sponge with the ingredients listed here – sieving the cocoa powder in with the flour – as instructed on page 24.

2. On baking paper dusted with cocoa powder roll and unroll the sponge from the long edge.

Make the ganache
1. Heat the double cream until just beginning to bubble. Remove from the heat and gently stir in the chocolate until melted, combined and smooth.

2. Leave aside to cool at room temperature until thick but still easily spreadable.

Make the filling
1. Whip the cream with the icing sugar and vanilla to medium peaks.

Assemble the yule log
1. Spread an even layer of cream over the cooled sponge and roll up into a spiral.

2. Cut a diagonal slice from the log about one to two fifths of its length. Use a little ganache to stick this to the side of the large section of the cake, to create a branch.

3. Cover the log in ganache; it is easiest to pipe the ganache on, then use a palette knife to spread it out evenly. Use a palette knife or a fork to create wavy patterns and lines, giving the log a bark-like appearance. Place the cake in the fridge to firm up.

4. Slice of the ends of the cake to reveal the spiral. Sprinkle over chopped nuts and dried fruit or candied peel to give a jewelled festive appearance, then lightly dust with icing sugar.

CHRISTMAS CROQUEMBOUCHE

INGREDIENTS

For the choux buns

2 quantities of choux pastry
and craquelin (page 17)
(gf)

For the crème pâtissière

400ml whole milk
4 large egg yolks
100g light brown sugar
40g cornflour
1 tablespoon vanilla bean
paste

**For the gingerbread
crème diplomat**

200ml double cream
20g light brown sugar
2 teaspoons ground
cinnamon
2 teaspoons ground ginger

**For the salted caramel
crème pâtissière**

1 quantity salted caramel
sauce (high butter and
low cream content)
(page 34)

**For the assembly
caramel**

300g caster sugar
30g glucose syrup or golden
syrup
50ml water
75g red, white and green
Christmas sprinkles (gf)

For the nougatine stand

1 quantity nougatine
(page 38)

At Christmas time, while it's dark outside, I love spending long hours in the kitchen. It's the perfect opportunity to get stuck into some project baking to create a grand showstopper like this croquembouche. Striking as it is, this is actually quite an achievable bake, especially if you use a cone mould as a guide to help build the choux tower straight. I used a 27cm tall polystyrene cone that cost just a couple of quid from a craft supplies shop.

Here, I set the croquembouche on a nougatine stand to give it a shape that evokes a Christmas tree, but this is not necessary. A free-standing croquembouche without the stand is still a remarkably impressive centrepiece for a Christmas-time table!

METHOD

Preheat the oven to 175°C fan/ 185°C conventional/gas mark 4.5. Line 2 baking trays with non-stick baking paper. Cut a large triangle of baking paper and wrap around an approximately 27cm tall polystyrene croquembouche cone, securing with a bit of Blu-Tack at the top and bottom.

Make the choux buns

1. Make the choux pastry as instructed on page 17. Pipe balls with about a 2cm diameter, leaving at least 3cm between each ball on the prepared baking sheets. (You might need more than 2 sheets or to do multiple batches to use up all the mixture.) Top with rounds of craquelin and bake for 30 to 35 minutes until deeply golden, risen and crisp. Use a piping nozzle to put a hole in the flat side of each bun and leave aside to cool.

2. You can make the choux buns up to 5 days in advance. If you do this, then on the day of the build it's best to reheat them at the same temperature for 5 minutes to dry them out and crisp them up again before filling.

Make the crème pat

1. Use the ingredients listed here to make a crème pat as outlined on page 46.

2. Split evenly between 2 bowls, cover with cling film and leave to cool at room temperature.

Make the gingerbread crème diplomat

1. Whisk the double cream with the sugar, cinnamon and ginger into medium peaks.

2. Beat a portion of cooled crème pat to loosen it off and fold through this whipped cream mix until you have one smooth mixture. Fill a piping bag with it and leave in the fridge until ready to use.

Make the salted caramel crème pat

1. Whisk the second portion of room temperature crème pat to loosen it off. Add in 200g of salted caramel sauce cooled to room temperature, and mix until combined. Fill a piping bag with this and chill in the fridge until ready to use.

Continues overleaf . . .

Fill the choux buns

1. Pipe half of the buns full with the gingerbread crème diplomat. Fill the other half with the salted caramel crème pat. Leave at least 5 choux buns unfilled.

Assemble the croquembouche cone

1. Fill a large deep bowl halfway with cold water. Fill a small bowl with some Christmas sprinkles to dip your choux buns into – you can refill this as you go along.

2. Add the caster sugar, glucose or golden syrup and water from the assembly caramel ingredients into a heavy-based pan. Stir over a high heat until the sugar has dissolved, leave over a high heat, swirling the pan occasionally until the mixture reaches a medium amber colour. Remove from the heat and dunk the pan base into the bowl of water to stop the caramel from colouring more. Remove from the water and place onto a heatproof surface.

3. Wearing sugar gloves to protect your hands, dip the tops of about 15 choux buns into the caramel, hold each one upside down out of the caramel for about 5 seconds to allow any excess to drip off, then dip the caramel-covered top in the Christmas sprinkles. Sit the bun sprinkle side up, and leave to set. The caramel should be fluid but is easiest to work with when it has enough viscosity to stick to the surface of the buns easily. If the sugar gets too firm to work with, place it back over a low heat, stirring to melt until it is workable again.

4. Lean one sprinkle-covered bun's flat side against the paper-lined cone. Dip the side of another choux bun in caramel and stick the caramel-coated side onto the side of the bun already in position. Repeat this process around the base level of the cone. Add another Christmas-sprinkle choux bun on the opposite side of the cone. Ensure the buns are tightly tucked in together. If you reach the end of the level and another bun won't fit, cut an unfilled bun to size and stick it in, so it fits snugly.

5. Repeat this process on the next level above. Dip 2 sides of the buns in caramel so you stick the buns to those on the level below and those side by side. Start by sticking a sprinkle-covered bun just to the left or right of the other sprinkle-covered buns on the layer below. Repeat this process for each layer, working up the cone until you reach the top, leaving an opening at the top.

6. Once you have covered the cone, leave the caramel to set hard. This should only take a few minutes. Carefully lift the cone off the base it is sitting on and even more carefully remove the cone from the inside of the croquembouche by pressing from the top of the cone and pulling it out from the bottom. Peel the baking paper away from the inside of the buns. You will now have a free-standing, hollow choux tower, an extraordinary centrepiece all on its own.

7. Finally, dip the bottom of a sprinkle-covered bun in caramel and place atop the croquembouche.

Make the nougatine stand

1. Lightly grease the outside of a 10cm cake tin with oil.

2. Make a batch of nougatine as detailed on page 38.

3. While warm, roll the nougatine out to a rectangle about 40cm long and 15cm wide. Use a sharp knife to cut a 38cm long rectangle with a width of 10cm or 1cm less than the height of the cake tin. While warm, mould this around the outside of your prepared tin. Leave to firm up for a few minutes then remove the nougatine cylinder from the tin.

4. Place the remaining offcuts in the oven at 150°C fan/160°C conventional/gas mark 3 for about 5 minutes until soft enough to work again. Roll this nougatine out and cut a 16cm circle out from it, using a cake tin or plate as a guide.

5. Make sure the cylinder stands flat. If it is doesn't, heat an empty pan on the hob and turn it upside down. Press the nougatine cylinder onto the pan's hot base to melt down the side that is too tall. Do this until you are happy that the cylinder is level.

Assemble the croquembouche

1. Place the nougatine circle onto the cylinder. Carefully lift the choux bun tower and place it onto the nougatine stand.

2. Surround the base of the tower with any leftover choux buns and additional Christmas bakes to look like an abundance of presents arranged under the tree!

A THANK YOU TO . . .

Mum, Dad, Andrew and Auntie Rachel. Thank you for the years of support of my baking, sharing my excitement while putting this book together and for being with me on the occasions when I allowed myself to get a little stressed.

For all my flatmates from the past two years, Jamie, Jacob, Ying, Abhi, Fraser, Rachel and Claudia. It's been an odd (but very fun) couple of years. I don't think you realise how much you mean to me and how much I have relied on your support. Thank you for keeping it fun. You're all the best.

I have to acknowledge my fellow bakers and all the Love Productions team, crew and staff involved in the Bake Off Bubble last year. They made it the best time of my life as a standalone experience, and I got to write this book as a result of that incredible summer. For many reasons, I am incredibly grateful for the experience and the input of everyone involved.

Seeing my recipes come to life through incredible photography has been one of the best parts of writing this book. Thank you, Susie, for the stunning photos and for helping make the long days of shooting a whole lot of fun.

Thanks also to Steve and Billy for letting us take over space at the beautiful Renaissance Club for photography.

For the team at Black & White Publishing, especially Ali. Thank you for affording me this opportunity, supporting me in continuing my studies alongside this project, and giving me the freedom to make this book exactly what I wanted it to be.

And for Anna and Geraldine at Yellow Poppy, thank you for the support.

Finally, a big thanks to you for picking up this copy. I hope you enjoy reading it and baking the recipes.

ABOUT PETER SAWKINS

Peter Sawkins, an accounting and finance student at the
University of Edinburgh, is the youngest ever winner of the
Great British Bake Off. A passionate baker since childhood,
he credits the show as one of the reasons he embarked on his
culinary journey. *Peter Bakes* is his first book.

You can find Peter on Instagram
@peter_bakes